DISCARD

RED, BROWN, AND BLACK DEMANDS
FOR BETTER EDUCATION

Red, Brown, and Black Demands for Better Education

by G. LOUIS HEATH

W
THE WESTMINSTER PRESS
Philadelphia

371.97
.H43¹R
C. 2

PUBLISHED BY THE WESTMINSTER PRESS ®
PHILADELPHIA, PENNSYLVANIA

PRINTED IN THE UNITED STATES OF AMERICA

For T. Bentley Edwards
and John U. Michaelis

Acknowledgments

I wish to thank Ivan Levin, field director of the Illinois Commission on Human Relations, for the invaluable assistance he rendered me during my research for the articles "Ghost Town Vigilantes: The Racial Pallor of Cairo," *The Nation*, Dec. 22, 1969; "Corrupt East St. Louis: Laboratory for Black Revolution," *The Progressive*, October, 1970; and, "Ghost Town," *The Nation*, May 24, 1971. These articles, the former two of which were a runner-up and a finalist in the Second and Third Annual Robert F. Kennedy Journalism Award competitions, appear in slightly revised form under the section entitled "Southern Illinois." The advice and information provided by the National Congress of American Indians and the Association on American Indian Affairs greatly facilitated my field research on the reservations. Generous access to the files of *El Malcriado*, the United Farm Workers Organizing Committee's newspaper, and the Social Protest Archives at the University of California's Bancroft Library proved indispensable. Finally, I must thank the editors of *The Nation, The Progressive, Interracial Review, Illinois Quarterly, Phi Delta Kappan, In-*

tegrated Education, and the *Journal of Secondary Education* who granted me permission to reprint my articles in this book.

G. L. H.

Contents

Introduction

An awareness, a consciousness of social plight among minorities, has spread across the land since the early '60s. The blacks, the largest minority group, were the first to attempt to act out their consciousness and make the world better for themselves. They have been followed lately by the Chicanos and finally the Indians. These three minorities have all made recent demands upon a social system that has discriminated greatly against them.

One of the foremost demands of these minorities has been that educational institutions serve them as well as the WASP majority. That is, they have aspired for education that provides a curriculum that is consistent with their identity and culture yet still teaches them the occupational skills to compete successfully in the marketplace. Where they have been unable to secure both relevance and skills in one educational package, they have often been frustrated into demanding either technical education that ignores their culture or cultural education that equips them with no viable skills. In one instance, they are vocationally trained but untutored in their culture and, in the other, they are culturally sensitized but unable to get a job. Both alternatives are dead ends for red, brown, and black learners and for American society. The hope is that the nation, despite all the apparent lack of common purpose, can still hear and act upon red, brown, and black demands that the schools both respect them culturally and train them for jobs. This book is dedicated to informing that hope.

I

RED DEMANDS
FOR BETTER EDUCATION

American Indians have become exceedingly defiant
in their demand for satisfying education. This defiance is
a part of the national Red Power Movement toward a
lasting, secure place in this society for tribal Americans.
The fish-ins in Washington State, the occupation of Mt.
Rushmore in South Dakota, and the Seneca appeal to
the United Nations to prevent the flooding of their
ancient lands in upstate New York are all expressions of
this movement. Perhaps the most symbolic and well-
known Red Power foray has been the occupation of
Alcatraz Island in San Francisco Bay. It is on Alcatraz
that the militancy and educational demands of America's
oppressed Indians seem most graphically expressed.

1

No Rock Is an Island[*]

On July 10, 1970, I went to the Alcatraz Receiving Depot at Pier 40 in San Francisco to sign up for a tour of Alcatraz Island, occupied, as is well known, by a hostile band of Indians. On November 20, 1969, the Indians had landed in small boats, claiming ownership under a one-hundred-year-old treaty that returned abandoned federal land to the Sioux nation. About eighty Indians have been living regularly on "The Rock" since the initial, serious invasion. (There was a nineteen-hour, sportive "invasion" before November 20.) The Government, after much hesitation, has finally announced it will demolish the cell blocks and other buildings on Alcatraz in order to establish a national park. Thomas E. Hannon, regional administrator of the General Services Administration, has indicated the GSA will transfer title to the twenty-one-acre island to the Department of the Interior, which will create the park. However, the Indians want to remain and develop the island as an Indian educational and cultural center. They are conducting tours, among other

[*] Originally appeared in *Phi Delta Kappan*, March, 1971, pp. 397–399. Reprinted by permission.

projects, for a limited number of non-Indians daily, in an effort to raise money for the center. Forty tourists are taken over daily: twenty at 10 A.M. and twenty at 1 P.M. I got a pass at 8:30 A.M. and, after scouting Fisherman's Wharf and Ghirardelli Square, boarded the Indians' boat, *Tubb* II, at 10 A.M. Minutes later I was gliding over churning riptides with nineteen other curious whites through a light smog (even San Francisco has readily detectable smog these days) toward The Rock, the national epicenter of the Indian protest movement.

Once on the island, location of the famous, fortresslike maximum security prison abandoned by the Government in 1963, I climbed steeply to the cell blocks, where the Indians were encamped. A major fire had recently caused considerable damage on the island. The fire was extraordinarily destructive because the Coast Guard had cut off electricity and water service to the island in an effort to unobtrusively force the tribes off the island. Destroyed were the warden's home, assistant warden's home—the Indians' makeshift hospital—and a three-apartment complex attached to the 214-foot light tower, gutted but tenaciously upright. The tower stood, I imagined, like a somber, prophetic totem pole.

What is the significance of Alcatraz?

Indian acreage has dwindled from 138 million in 1887 to 50 million today. "By nabbing this site," smiles John, a twenty-three-year-old Sioux, "we've just reversed the process." "It's the best thing that's happened to Indian unity since Little Bighorn," exults an Apache. "It's our Statue of Liberty," claims a Comanche. The Alcatraz walls are profusely scrawled with tribal hieroglyphics and signs such as "This Land Is My Land" and "Custer

Had It Coming." The direct redress of grievances for stolen land and broken treaties is undoubtedly the foremost significance of Alcatraz.

Independent of the symbolism of Alcatraz, that the red man will no longer stoically endure privation and theft, the vision of an Indian educational and cultural center for Alcatraz is the most salient invention to emerge from the invasion. The invaders want an Indian educational and cultural complex on Alcatraz that will include a center for native American studies, spiritual center, ecology center, Indian training school, and American Indian museum. They also aspire to found, as a supportive program, an Indian traveling university to minister to the educational needs of all tribes. They believe an Indian educational center is a *sine qua non* for the preservation of a resilient Indian culture. Recognized national Indian leadership, particularly Jack Forbes [1] and Lehman Brightman, point to the fact that blacks, Jews, Catholics, and the various Protestant denominations enjoy their own educational institutions. Every ethnic and racial group, save the Indians, can also relate to relatively autonomous societal traditions and culturally expressive universities operative in ancestral countries. But the Indians have no such resources. Their identity is very gravely threatened by the lack of a secure, geographically distinct parent culture to compensate for their highly tenuous situation as a vanquished people here. Indians are now attempting to guarantee their historic life by asserting their Indianness. They apparently intend to invest much Red Power in educational populism as a vehicle for realizing tribal continuity.

John Folster, vice-president of the Bay Area Native

American Council, representing twenty-eight Indian organizations, interprets the Alcatraz occupation as a costly, but effective, public relations venture:

> It [Alcatraz] has given us an opportunity for the first time to bring to the world the true picture of our desolation. It is a peaceful effort. It has hurt no one but the Indians themselves, who have sacrificed much to compel the Government to recognize their rights to land, education, decent houses, and jobs.

Another Alcatraz Indian, a Sioux, stresses the Indians' determination to achieve their objectives:

> We are willing to negotiate on money and time the day they will turn over the deed to the island. That is all that is negotiable. There will be no park on this island because it changes the whole meaning of what we are here for.
>
> The American Government reacted swiftly, for a change. They announced their plans to make Alcatraz part of a Golden Gate National Recreation Area. They claimed the Alcatraz section would focus on the theme of "Indian contributions" to American life. But we will no longer be museum pieces and tourist attractions. We want Alcatraz for our own educational and cultural center.

A contingent of Indians has even organized a war council on The Rock in the hope of thwarting the Government's plans to convert the former prison island into a national park: "We are going to dig in and go ahead with our plans to build an Indian cultural center," threatens Joseph L. Morris, fifty-three, a Blackfoot leader from Montana. "We're going ahead with our own damn plans. We're not going to leave until we get what we came here for."

From the Indians' painful consciousness of tribal self, turned outward into activism, has crystallized the saving admission that, in the long term, struggle requires intellectual nurture, if it is to be more than frenetic and abortive Sisyphean perplexity. An Indian educational and cultural center would cast into enduring scholarship and teaching the Indians' image of self and culture. It is this codification of the Indian dialectic that would ultimately guarantee sanctuary for the Indian spirit. Self-affirming education is the only viable method for tribal Americans to defend themselves.

THE AQUATIC PARK POW-WOW

The following Sunday I attended an Indian rally in San Francisco's Aquatic Park. A large crowd, heavily Indian, sat on the stone steps facing Alcatraz Island as Indians from seventy tribes authenticated their spiritual unity. Buffy Sainte-Marie, famed Cree folk singer, a great spirit in a tiny, black-haired frame, sang. Between songs, she rapped a bit. "We ask for your help," she said. "The thing we are not asking for any more is permission." While Buffy sang, Indians sold posters reading, "Alcatraz Is Not an Island," to obtain cash nutrient for the Alcatraz invaders' financial malnutrition. Bernie Whitebear, chairman of the United Indians of All Tribes, pleased the multitude: "Alcatraz is the beginning of a new revolution for the American Indian." John Trudell, of the United Indians of All Tribes on Alcatraz, emphasized that "the problem in America today is the system

which is geared to meet only white needs." That seemed
to be the bitter, red nationalist consensus—that Indians
do not fit into the prevailing order. Alcatraz is their attempt to liberate what they feel is an imprisoned society
that obtains both sadistic pleasure and material advantage through the oppression of the Indian.

Fred, a Yakima Indian participant in the "pow-wow,"
informed me: "The battle won't be won or lost on Alcatraz. It is a good place to start; it is a fine symbol as well
as a beautiful reality, but it's just the beginning." If
the Indians of All Tribes on Alcatraz can make the future, their occupation is indeed just the beginning. They
painted on cowhide the past summer their own deed for
Alcatraz. The leathery document proclaims that ". . . we
shall exercise dominion and all rights of use and posses-
sion over Alcatraz Island in San Francisco Bay," and
that "from time to time" Indians elsewhere in the country will "announce the restoration of other land to Indian
dominion."

The warning to expect further Indian seizures of federal land hints at the fulfillment of a prophecy spoken
in February, 1970, by Chief Eagle Feather, a Sioux medicine man in South Dakota: "At the end of ten years,
Indians will have an equal place with white men. At the
end of ten years we will have our sacred ground and
sweat lodge on the extreme East Coast."

If the ethos of Alcatraz persists and Eagle Feather is
truly a prophet, there will be Indian educational centers
as well on the eastern skirt of the American continent.
The ineluctable reality is that militancy and educational
renaissance are both requisite to a regeneration of Indian culture.

Education is most legitimately revolution and refor-

mation, preferably of a continuing sort. In the absence
of perpetual change, a haggard, near-destitute band of
Indians has forced a confrontation with the most powerful government on earth. It seeks a merciful transformation of policy. Its heresy has been to capture Alcatraz for
genuine human need and betterment, for education that
venerates the Indian citizen's identity, rather than leaving it to crumble as a desolate, abandoned prison. The
Rock is more than an island, not only for Indians, but for
all mankind. Only when we create educational and cultural centers on all our Alcatrazes will the school and
society be humanized in full measure. The gaunt Alcatraz Indians are most aware of this cosmic parameter because they have suffered unspeakable incursions upon
their humanity. In a global village, where no rock can
qualify as an island, the diminishment of one is the
desecration of all. And therein resides the ultimate imperative for and significance of an Indian educational
and cultural center on Alcatraz.

Tragically, the Federal Government has not responded
constructively to the Alcatraz Indians' demand for better life and education. On June 11, 1971, as I compiled
this book, armed federal marshals recaptured the island
and forcibly evicted the Indians. U.S. Attorney James L.
Browning, Jr., informed me that a "protective force" of
marshals will be stationed on the island to prevent
further occupations. Chain link fences will also be
erected and trained dogs will be used to patrol the shore-
line. At a subsequent press conference, Browning stressed
that "removal of the illegal inhabitants had become an
urgent necessity since the Coast Guard was prohibited
from restoring inoperative navigational aids." Conve-

nience for the majority has finally taken precedence over the rights and cultural integrity of the red minority on Alcatraz. The dramatic event is over, but the idea of the conquered, defiled Indian attaining to full dignity in American society will not die easily. The embers of the once-dying, ancient, tribal council fires have been stirred too vigorously for that. There will be many more Alcatrazes and there will be genuine Indian education or there will be no more American society.

NOTE

1. Jack D. Forbes, "An American Indian University: A Proposal for Survival," *Journal of American Indian Education*, January, 1966, pp. 1–2.

2

The Life and Education
of the American Indian *

American Indians number only 600,000 and are scat-
tered over twenty-eight states.[1] Two thirds of the Indians reside on reservations where the Bureau of Indian
Affairs administers educational and welfare services to
them in fulfillment of treaty obligations.[2] The Bureau
binds its charges into a web of paternalism and discrimination. Most of the other Indians are integrated
into the economic underworld of the cities, where they
stoically endure privation and cultural shock far from
the reservations. The urban Indian experiences the abuse
that is doubly the lot of the poor and nonwhite.

I visited fourteen reservations and one settlement in
the Southwest, Midwest, West, and Pacific Northwest
during the summer of 1970, interviewing 147 Indians
and other persons somehow knowledgeable or prejudiced
in the matter of Indian affairs. My field research provides the substance for this section's observations.

* Originally appeared in *The Illinois Quarterly*, Vol. 33, No. 3
(February, 1971). Reprinted in edited form by permission.

THE CONFLICT OF CULTURES

The Indian pupil's communal identity clashes with the school's emphasis on competition and individual rewards. The Indian becomes deeply abashed when he excels. He deliberately fails rather than embarrass his classmates. When a teacher endeavors to goad an Indian student into rivalry, he suddenly becomes "shy and stupid." The school, representing the mainstream values, seeks to assimilate the Indian pupil rather than respect his identity and accommodate him in the curriculum. It rhetorically expounds the vaunted pluralism of America, but refuses to practice it in the classroom. Culturally myopic teacher behavior produces a strongly denigratory impact upon the Indian child. The experience of the Mesquakie children is particularly revealing in this regard. In Iowa's South Tama County District, where a few Mesquakie children attend classes, a teacher raised the issue of taxes in a class that included four Mesquakie students. One of the Mesquakies contributed to the ensuing discussion and the teacher responded by berating him: "You Indians don't pay taxes. You're so lazy you have to live off the Government." In another instance, a teacher informed the Mesquakie children that they would not be allowed to produce any Indian art in school. The tribal leaders had no alternative (excluding cultural suicide) but to rent a deserted farmhouse so their children could paint and draw in the Mesquakie tradition.[3]

The standard, mediocre teacher in the BIA schools is particularly adept at impugning the cultural integrity of Indian students.[4] Classes often begin with the Lord's Prayer. Some teachers, notably on the Navajo Reservation and at the St. Mary's School for Indian Girls in Springfield, South Dakota, even advocate the free labor of Indian girls in their homes (scrubbing floors, doing laundry, and the like) for the instructional purpose of "teaching the American way of housekeeping." They individualize instruction with such courses as "Laundry" and "Cleaning." [5] This sort of fundamental violation of human rights is especially grievous when one considers that Indians exercise no voice in educational decisions. They elect no school board members in either the public school districts or the BIA school jurisdictions. The public schools even receive Johnson-O'Malley Act money for their Indian pupils, [6] but they do not expend the federal money to satisfy their Indian charges' distinctive educational needs. The funds accrue insufferable interest as coercive assimilation capital.

The BIA schools function more like child labor and detention camps than educational institutions. The Bureau spends $1,500 on each of the 35,000 Indian pupils housed in the boarding schools. [7] The per capita expenditure must cover a child's entire living and educational expenses for ten months. Such funding affords only elementary institutional care. The available education is simply vocational training that is a by-product of BIA *in loco parentis:* the officials require able students to perform maintenance and repair work on buildings and equipment, particularly carpentry and painting, to help defray operating expenses. Cursory, noninstructional supervision of Indian child labor is intended to legitimize the deception as genuine vocational training. The subterfuge is preposterous: 10,000 Indians annually receive training that has no market value while there are only seven doctors, four lawyers, and two engineers who are

Indians in the entire United States.[8] The inference that BIA education does not prepare Indian students to improve the Indian community is empirically valid.

When additional money becomes available for Indian education, it is often spent foolishly. For example, the Government paid Westinghouse Electric $2 million to provide experimental computer-aided instruction for fifteen Menominee children in Wisconsin. Although the funds were adequate to supply conventional quality education to every Menominee child, the 900 other Menominee pupils remained trapped in a condition of enforced educational austerity while the Government subsidized Westinghouse Electric's research into a potentially lucrative market.[9]

The BIA's pursuit of assimilation is basically a rationalization of the exploitation, decimation, and attempted genocide the white man has organized against the Indian. The historic assumption is that the redskin's culture and character are too defective for him to succeed independently. The schools, the national instruments of acculturation, must integrate the Indian into white culture so he can transcend his innate (whether by culture or by genes) inferiority. This is the racist myth of "compensatory education." It includes a panoply of pseudoscientific terms like the "culturally deprived" and, more recently, the "socially disadvantaged." Beyond the abstruse verbiage and cultural blind spots, one can detect a sophisticated white racism: Indians must be enriched with the elixir of life, the cure-all of the downtrodden (to paraphrase the frontier mountebank's spiel), and the happy tonic is white folkways and education.

ASSIMILATION AS WHITE SUPREMACY

It is not at all obscure that undergirding the super-structure of assimilation is the doctrine of white supremacy. Thus, in a recent history of the Cherokees, an Oklahoma author writes of the "full-bloods," the genetically pure Indians: "They supplement their small income from farms and subsidies from the Government with wage work or seasonal jobs in nearby towns or on farms belonging to white men. . . . Paid fair wages, this type of worker usually spends his money as quickly as he makes it on whiskey, and on cars, washing machines, and other items that, uncared for, soon fall into necessitous disuse." [10] Contrary to that assertion, the Indians are not "paid fair wages." It is my observation that white employers often pay Indians extremely low wages and aver that they are, in fact, performing a millennial missionary work. They claim they provide employment and guidance for an infantile people, too ingenuous to manage for themselves. The BIA employs the same ethic in cunningly commandeering the vestiges of tribal government, including the disbursement of the Indians' own funds to the Indians. For example, the Papagos of Southern Arizona applied for some of their money when a heavy snowfall threatened their livestock. By the time the request had worked its way through bureaucratic channels, two thousand head of cattle had starved to death.[11] White supremacy and bureaucratic inertia have, *in tandem,* inflicted relentless hardship on the Indian. Cherokee anthropologist Robert Thomas concludes that the BIA is "the most complete colonial system in the world." [12]

White exploitative paternalism has produced the intensely negative self-concept the Indian suffers. The Coleman Report disclosed that American Indians experience more stigma and self-hatred than any other ethnic group.[13] The very process of growing up is absurd for the Indian because it is anti-Indian. The Indians attach little value to themselves, a response inculcated by a school system that infects the children with a virulent form of white racism. The Indian's excessive school dropout rate, his depressing suicide statistics (the teen-age rate is over ten times the national average),[14] and his extravagant alcoholism are shameful indicators of the defamatory influences impinging on him. Until recently, no remedy has been in the offing. But the Indian's new antidote for white oppression and the resultant feelings of powerlessness and self-hatred is political organization. He has begun to seriously countervail white discrimination through the National Congress of American Indians, founded in 1944, and regional and local groups. The insidious bite of paternalism has become accordingly less toxic.

Contemporary Indian education is neither Indian nor education. Indian pupil achievement and dropout rates reflect the utter meaninglessness and irrelevance of what passes for education in the BIA schools and the public schools to which many Indians have been transferred. A quarter of the teachers who instruct Indian children admit they would rather teach someone else.[15] Even the job descriptions of the federal boarding schools betray their real purpose: "attendant," "matron," and "guard" are occupational categories for penal and mental institutions—not schools. Bureaucratic absurdities subject Indian pupils to unnecessary misery and anguish. Two hundred and sixty-seven Alaskan Eskimos, who speak no Midwestern Indian language or passable words of English, have been transferred five thousand miles to Chilocco boarding school in Oklahoma.[16] It is disturbingly apparent that Chilocco will not meet their learning needs. The Indian pupils at Chilocco who can understand English are perhaps even more unfortunate, for they can ingest the emetic pabulum that is provided. For example, I saw a cavalry-and-Indian film being shown in one of the Chilocco dormitories. According to the usual format, the Army was heavily outnumbered and held a militarily untenable position. The Indians, assaulting the position, were being killed, one every shot. As they were on the verge of overwhelming the Army troops, a bugle sounded and the cavalry charged to the rescue from behind a hill. The Indian pupils cheered the climax, inadvertently divulging the utter alienation of their education.

The insipid paternalism that induces Indian alienation is evident in the BIA's pamphlet *Curriculum Needs of Navajo Pupils*. From it we learn that the Navajo child "needs to begin to develop knowledge of how the dominant culture is pluralistic and how many people worked to become the culture which is the American mainstream of life . . ."; "needs to understand that every man is free to rise as high as he is able and willing . . ."; "needs assistance with accepting either the role of leader or follower . . ."; "needs to understand that a mastery of the English language is imperative to compete in the world today . . ."; and "needs to understand that work is necessary to exist and succeed." This manifesto of the American way of life, albeit commendable as a doctrine, completely ignores the fact that there is also an American Indian way of life, as sacred and viable as the mainstream cultural tradition. This cultural insensitivity is exceedingly debilitating to Indian youngsters. Many learn virtually nothing from the white teacher who clings to the antiquated teaching methods and ideas of nineteenth-century Middle America. For example, I learned through interviews that at Point Arena, California, white children and the Kashaya Pomo children from the depressed Stewart's Point Reservation attend school together in a climate of intense enmity. The white children habitually challenge Kashaya Pomo children to fights and taunt them mercilessly. The teachers cannot comprehend why the Indians will not behave and toil assiduously on their lessons. They do not realize that few Kashaya youngsters command a working knowledge of English, that the only cues the Kashaya pupils can effectively read are nonverbal, and that quite often those cues happen to be physical insults. The eventual result is that the Kashaya pupils drop out. The "push out" process has been so thorough that no Kashaya child has completed high school in the past five years, I was told.

The Indian child, initially quick-learning, well-adjusted, and eager, does well the first few years of school, achieving commensurably with white children. But the "crossover phenomenon" soon sets in. The Indian pupil begins to regress rapidly between the fifth and seventh grades. For example, a study of the Stewart Institute in Carson City, Nevada, shows that Indian sixth-graders score 5.2 on the California Achievement Test, but score only 8.4 six years later at graduation. The national achievement test average for Indian high school graduates is only the 9.5 grade level.[17] This figure is all the more disconcerting when one considers that 60 percent of all Indian students do not graduate, but drop out somewhere along the lockstep hierarchy. The typical Indian completes about five years of schooling. The implicit policy is to pass students on until they either graduate or drop out. The ineluctable inference is that the schools actually impair the Indians whom they purport to educate, inflicting severe psychic damage. Educators persist in forcing a square peg into a round hole, despite all the lamentable signs that compulsory assimilation is more alienation than education.

BOARDING SCHOOL LIFE

The nonacademic aspects of the federal boarding schools offer no improvement upon the dismal classroom situation. The student's life is regimented by a near-military discipline. In fact, the schools resemble military installations: each is a complex of deteriorating, one-color buildings, the shabby sentinels of the minds and spirits of America's Indian children. A number of condemned buildings are in use, notably at Chilocco, Oklahoma, Tuba City, Arizona, and Fort Wingate, New Mexico. The Brookings Institution's 1928 Meriam Report pointed specifically to the preposterousness of operating Fort Wingate as an elementary boarding school. But forty-two years later, the practice continues.[18]

The impersonal, indecorous, and bleak living conditions of the BIA schools in no way replicate a healthy home environment. The dormitories, with their long rows of double-decked iron beds, are strikingly similar to military barracks. I saw iron bars enclosing dormitory windows in several schools, exposing, it seems to me, administrators' distrust of the students and one of the institution's real functions. Most significantly, the school treats

everyone identically: each child is repressed into a stultifying conformity. The monolithic process dehumanizes,
acting upon each child as if he were an inanimate object.
The school programs each hour of the pupil's day into an
invariable routine of classes, study halls, meals, chores,
and recreation. Rule violators receive demerits that can
be expunged by doing extra work or sacrificing privileges. Students at some schools may even be severely
beaten or handcuffed for extended periods of time.[19]
Punishments often become very physical at Fort Wingate, Tuba City, Northern Cheyenne, and the Intermountain Indian School in Utah. For example, Intermountain
matrons duck the heads of Indian children suspected of
drinking into unclean toilets.[20] The confidential statements of two teachers and three attendants at these four
schools, in addition to the undisguised reality of seven
children walking about with arms in slings, suggests that
much more "discipline" may be operative than cursory
investigation can ascertain.

Boys and girls endure a strict segregation in the boarding schools. They deeply resent the isolation and retaliate
by making clandestine social contacts that often lead
precipitously to premature sexual relations. School officials severely discipline students who defy the sexual repression policy. They seem to believe that sexuality among
Indians is a sin. The superintendent at Chilocco even
wants to construct a jail and employ additional guards
to handle the transgressors of the sexual separatist code.[21]

The boarding schools discourage visits. If a visitor does
appear, he is dissuaded from talking to the children. The
school officials claim visits and conversation render the
children hyperactive, particularly if a visitor happens to
be a parent. Runaways always seem to increase after

visits. Stirred from sensory deprivation, the Indian child
seeks out further attention. Since he cannot secure it in
the dormitories where one matron attends one hundred or
more children, he flees his desperate condition. To obviate the upheaval that contact with the outside world en-
genders, the policy of discouraging visits has become so
entrenched at the Fort Wingate school that a sign over a
dormitory entrance officially deprecates parental visits.
If this deterrent does not work, the often impracticable,
always obstructive road to Wingate provides a second
line of defense. Wingate is exemplary. I am forced to
the conclusion that the objective of the entire boarding
school system is to narcotize and arrest the young Indian's developing mind and emotions so that he will not
become a troublemaker.

The boarding schools deny the cultural identity of the
Indian. School employees exercise great care to address
the Indian children only in English. They scathingly cen-
sure the speaking of native languages in both the class-
rooms and the dormitories. This cultural bleaching has
been insensately effective. For example, the Indian dormitory attendant scrupulously avoids demonstrating any
knowledge of his tribal language. He is religiously convinced that knowing it is shameful, that it is an incubus
of inferiority. He represents perhaps the most consum-
mate example of how white-manipulated education de-
files the Indian. He is the quintessence of the BIA's "assimilated Indian." Many run away or commit suicide in
desperate efforts to assert their dignity, but the attendant
has overcome all the degrading obstacles, repressing any
tormenting uncertainty he may have about the purpose
of his education. He eventually embraces the education
the "Great White Father" has provided and assumes the

ambivalent status of an "Uncle Tomahawk." He is the inimitable product of the boarding school system.

The young, idealistic teachers, including a sizable contingent of VISTA volunteers, who gravitate to the BIA schools, become rapidly disenchanted. Their commitment to effective change threatens bureaucratic equilibrium. Once identified as potential disrupters of the *status quo*, the BIA officials paternalize them much as they do the Indians: they implement a panoply of stinging stratagems to extinguish creative and enthusiastic involvement in the educational process. For example, one Navajo Reservation teacher, a former Peace Corps volunteer, told the Senate Subcommittee on Indian Education that her principal frequently discredited the Indian students in the presence of teachers with statements such as "All Navajos are brain-damaged," and "Navajo culture belongs in a museum." [22] Those who do not leave, disgusted with the cultural assassination and impertinent desecration of teacher professionalism, survive by defecting to the role of eight-to-five bureaucrats and somehow becoming inured to their students' crying needs. The statistical consequence of this negative selectivity is that the turnover rate among BIA teachers is double the national average.[23] To the Indian pupils, the teacher is a stranger passing through. He is a stranger not simply because his sojourn is short-lived, but also for the reason that he is very seldom Indian. Only 16 percent of the Bureau's teachers are Indian.[24] The white teachers, even if they are genuinely concerned about the welfare of their students, seldom command sufficient tribal knowledge and ethnic empathy to relate seriously classroom activities to Indian life and culture. An Interior Department report systematically documented this failure in Alaska, finding

that "education which gives the Indian, Eskimo and
Aleut knowledge of—and therefore pride in—their historic and cultural heritage is almost nonexistent. . . .
In the very few places where such an attempt is made,
it is poorly conceived and inadequate." [25] The cultural
deficiency of the curriculum might be remedied if more
Indians taught, but this is an unlikely development since
very few Indians graduate from college. Perhaps more
paraprofessionals could play a decisive role.

Indian students often react to their dehumanizing
living conditions and schooling by committing suicide.
For example, twelve of 240 students in the Northern
Cheyenne Reservation's Busby School attempted suicides
in a recent eighteen-month period.[26] A sixteen-year-old
boy, charged with drinking in school, committed suicide
in jail at Fort Hall, Idaho.[27] A Crow boy apparently
drank himself to death at Chilocco boarding school.[28] A
Sioux boy hanged himself in the Wilkin County jail at
Breckenridge, Minnesota, in December, 1968. He had
been held "in virtual isolation," according to a newspaper
report, for seven weeks. Only thirteen, he had been accused of complicity in a car theft. No court hearing had
been granted during his incarceration.[29] Dr. Daniel
O'Connell testified before the Senate Subcommittee on
Indian Education that "the situation as far as suicide is
concerned is especially acute among the boarding school
children, particularly in high school." [30] Unfortunately,
the self-immolations do not represent isolated incidents,
but fit into a comprehensive pattern of hopelessness and
self-estrangement.

Running away, psychoanalytically quite difficult to dis-
tinguish from suicide, is another of the Indian student's
historic responses to the schools. In 1891, three Kiowa

schoolboys froze to death trying to reach home in a blizzard.[31] Indian students still perish in institutional escapes. For example, two Navajo boys recently froze to death attempting to reach their parents fifty miles away and a young, very drunk runaway froze to death at the Albuquerque Boarding School.[32] The impulse to flee is intense among students detained in the boarding schools. The absurdity of their predicament intrudes into consciousness in more aware moments. The agonizing self-admission of living an alien life impels them to abscond, departing the educational limbo that confines them.

TERMINATION AND THE "MELTING POT"

"Termination," the phasing out of the reservations and the liquidation of the Indian land base, would irreparably shatter Indian communities. American whites exist as atoms in the maws of urban behemoths called megalopolises. They take umbrage at any community, whether Amish, Orthodox Jewish, or Indian, that seeks to hang on to a strand of common humanity among men. Everyone should be an "individual"; so, terminate the reservations. The unhospitalized paranoia over community has incited the destruction or drastic erosion of virtually every ethnic enclave. (A few colorful trappings displayed on the old country's national holidays and infrequent, halting words of Polish or whatever do not constitute tenacious ethnicity.) The Indians seem unwilling to heed the cues as to where rewards reside and how punishments are meted out. They persist in their Indianism.

The present wholesale transfer of Indian students into the public schools, begun in 1965, signifies a powerful impetus toward termination and detribalization.[33] Two thirds of all Indian students on the reservations have already been transferred to schools that have no idea how to educate them.[34] Very few tribes are sufficiently powerful and political to contest independently the indiscriminate one-way busing. (One group of Navajos claims, "The buses are kidnaping our children.") The Mesquakie Tribe has perhaps most effectually challenged the federal bureaucracy's unilateral actions. They initiated legal procedures to enjoin the BIA from closing their settlement school [35] and transferring all their children to public schools. The regional BIA officials in Minneapolis had become so accustomed to Indian compliance that, when the Mesquakies reacted, they spent several confused days determining a revised policy. Don Wanatee, secretary of the Mesquakie Tribal Council, flatly asserts, "We want the Mesquakie people to operate the school the way they see it." Most threatened tribes have been unable to translate this spirit of participation into purposeful action.

Termination would be tantamount to the abrogation of the Government's Indian treaty obligations. It would supply the final solution to the Indian problem. When the Indians relinquished their lands, the Federal Government signed treaties promising to protect their rights and provide essential services, such as schools and hospitals. These pacts precluded the populist fundamentalists in state and local jurisdictions from inflicting their prejudices upon the "naked savages." The anti-Indian crusaders have been obliged to direct their fervid antagonism through the BIA, which all too often has not altogether fulfilled its guardianship role, but has undoubtedly functioned historically as a significant buffer against avaricious and opportunistic predators. Without the BIA, the reservations long ago would have passed into private ownership and unscrupulous entrepreneurs would have defrauded the Indians of all their alienable properties. Yet today, the BIA's termination policy promises the ultimate depredation that the special interests have been craving for decades.

A majority of white Americans look askance at the Indian. The Indian stress on cooperation and community over competition and possessiveness seems singularly un-American. A white man in Ponca City, Oklahoma, who dresses as an Indian to entertain tourists, shared his expertise: "All they do is sit out there on the reservations waiting to be fed." The charlatan's attitude, especially in view of his unique, seasonal occupation, caricatures white prejudice: exploit the Indian but deny him dignity since he is not really an American. He lives for the community while we, "the Americans" (the supreme ethnocentric arrogation), live for ourselves. Termination of the reservations would force the Indian into the self-interested mainstream and fulfill the "melting pot" prophecy, but it would kill the Indian forever.

Anti-Indian prejudice intensifies as one approaches an Indian reservation. On the Northern Cheyenne Reservation in Montana, a truck driver confided to me, "This state would be a helluva lot better off if we didn't have to take care of so many damned lazy Indians." In Toppenish, Washington, a storekeeper noted that "the Indians waste a lot of our good land just sitting around." In Ponca City, Oklahoma, a realtor opined that "the Indians ought to stop drinking, get off their duffs, and do some work." [36] A shameless sign in front of a general store and gasoline station near the Pine Ridge Reservation in South Dakota restricts its clientele, advising "No Dogs or Indians Allowed." These attitudes are not isolated from local public policy, especially law enforcement. The arrest rate for Indians in towns near reservations is thirty times the rate for whites and six times the rate for blacks.[37] It is little wonder that the Indian has begun to experience an unsettling paranoia. Every force seems to work against his cultural survival. He has witnessed the tragic termination of the Menominee and Klamath Reservations. His most apprehensive and pessimistic inferences do not lack substance.

The plight of the 11,000 Oglala Sioux at Pine Ridge Reservation is typical of the permanent depression that afflicts Indians. About half the families live in small huts covered with boards, sod, or rusted sheet metal. Floors are of tamped earth. A good 90 percent of the huts have no plumbing or electricity. A few families live in abandoned auto bodies and chicken coops. Most Oglala Sioux must somehow haul water—as much as twelve miles, depending upon their location on the reservation. No bank, hotel, drugstore, or theater—none of the appurtenances of twentieth-century life—embellish the reservation. The unemployment rate among the Oglala varies, but averages about 75 percent, hitting a peak of 95 percent in winter.[38] One of the grim anomalies of the Oglala is that sixty-four research projects in progress command an aggregate funding sufficient to solve many of the reservation's problems.[39]

The situation at Pine Ridge is not at all unrepresentative of other reservations. The appalling poverty of the peoples of Asia and Africa is the norm. Over 75 percent of the housing on the reservations is substandard, with 50 percent beyond repair.[40] A recent survey on twenty-two reservations showed that the water was 80 to 100 percent contaminated and more than 70 percent of the water had to be carried a mile or more.[41] Owing to such primitive living conditions, the reservation Indian is eight times as likely to be infected with hepatitis, seven times as likely to contract tuberculosis, and three times as likely to die of pneumonia and influenza as the non-Indian.[42] In fact, one of every five Indian deaths is attributable to preventable diseases that afflict the reservations on an epidemic scale.[43] The cumulative, toxic effects of misery, want, and high morbidity cut the Indian's life-span short by one third of the white's. The Indian lives a harsh, primitive forty-four years in a preindustrial subculture; the white, reaping the harvest of the scientific and cybernetic revolutions, is privileged to a comfortable sixty-seven years.[44] Callous WASP values have produced the cruel discrepancy.

The life and education of the American Indian are, according to many sources, certainly dehumanizing processes. The red demand has been for more humanism in life and education, as we discussed in the previous section. The degree the desired reformation has come to the schools concerns us next.

NOTES

1. Lehman Brightman, "Red Power," *The Black Politician,* Vol. I, No. 2 (October, 1969), p. 37. *The Black Politician* is a journal published by the Center on Urban and Minority Affairs, 955 South Western Avenue, Los Angeles, Calif. 90006.

2. Information provided in a letter from the Bureau of Indian Affairs, National Headquarters, Washington, D.C., June 4, 1970.

3. These incidents were reported to the author in personal interviews with Indians in the community.

4. See the whole of the following: Stan Steiner, *The*

New Indians (Harper & Row, Publishers, Inc., 1968); Edgar S. Cahn (ed.), *Our Brother's Keeper: The Indian in White America* (The World Publishing Company, 1969); and Vine Deloria, Jr., *Custer Died for Your Sins: An Indian Manifesto* (The Macmillan Company, 1969). There are a number of examples of culturally callous teacher behavior in these volumes.

5. Peter Collier, "The Red Man's Burden," *Ramparts,* Vol. VIII, No. 8 (February, 1970), p. 28.

6. The Johnson-O'Malley Act is intended to provide money specifically for satisfying the distinctive educational needs of Indian pupils.

7. Dr. Carl Marburger, commissioner of education for the State of New Jersey, former assistant commissioner for the Bureau of Indian Affairs, data furnished at the hearings before the Subcommittee on Indian Education of the Committee on Labor and Public Welfare, United States Senate, Ninety-First Congress, First Session on Policy, Organization, Administration, and New Legislation Concerning the American Indian, Part 1, February 18, 19, 24, and March 27, 1969; April 11, 1969, Fairbanks, Alaska (U.S. Government Printing Office, 1969), p. 315. The 2,371 pages of testimony transcribed in 1969 before the Subcommittee on Indian Education, the "Kennedy Committee," support the allegation that the education provided the Indian is extremely corrosive. The subcommittee's final report, published in November, 1969, offers sixty recommendations for "culturally sensitive" and bilingual programs and Indian participation in educational decision-making to neutralize the contemporary caustic curriculum.

8. Lehman Brightman, president, United Native Americans, San Francisco, data presented at the hearings before the Subcommittee on Indian Education, *ibid.,* p. 33.

9. "Fifteen Little Indians: Westinghouse Computer Project on Menominee Reservation," *The New Republic,* June 17, 1967, p. 6.

10. Quoted in Albert L. Wahraftig and Robert K. Thomas, "Renaissance and Repression: The Oklahoma Cherokee," *Trans-Action*, Vol. VI (February, 1969), pp. 45–46.

11. "Deadly Windfall: Navajo Tribe Suffers from Snowfall," *Time*, Jan. 5, 1968, p. 23.

12. Collier, *loc. cit.*, p. 31.

13. James S. Coleman *et al.*, *Equality of Educational Opportunity* (U.S. Government Printing Office, 1966), pp. 288, 322, and 324.

14. Brightman, "Red Power," p. 38.

15. Coleman *et al.*, *op. cit.*, pp. 317–319.

16. Daniel Henninger and Nancy Esposito, "Regimented Non-Education: Indian Schools," *The New Republic*, March, 1968, p. 18.

17. Collier, *loc. cit.*, p. 31.

18. Henninger and Esposito, *loc. cit.*, p. 20.

19. "Official Horror Story of Federally-Run Chilocco Indian School," *Integrated Education*, Vol. VII, No. 4 (July–August, 1969), pp. 48–51. The report concludes that "there is evidence of criminal malpractice, not to mention physical and mental perversion, by certain staff members." It notes that "youngsters reported they were handcuffed for as long as 18 hours in the dormitory . . . or chained to a basement pillar or from a suspended pipe. One team member . . . verified a youngster's hurt arms, the deformed hands of another boy, and an obviously broken rib of another."

20. Letter from Intermountain School employee to the Citizens Advocate Center, Washington, D.C., March 2, 1969. The letter writer reports that one employee "dunks the students' heads into a toilet bowl which is unfit for even a hand."

21. Interview with a confidentially disgusted teacher at the Chilocco Indian School.

22. Collier, *loc. cit.*, p. 31.

23. Dr. Alan Sorkin, economist in residence, Brookings Institution, Washington, D.C., data presented at the hear-

ings before the Subcommittee on Indian Education, *op. cit.*, p. 330.

24. Henninger and Esposito, *loc. cit.*, p. 19.

25. *Ibid.*

26. *Ibid.*, p. 21.

27. William Brandon, "The American Indians: The Un-Americans," *The Progressive,* Vol. XXXIV, No. 1 (January, 1970), p. 37. Mr. Brandon is the author of *The American Heritage Book of Indians.*

28. Henninger and Esposito, *loc. cit.*, p. 21.

29. Brandon, *loc. cit.*, p. 38.

30. Henninger and Esposito, *loc. cit.*, p. 21.

31. Brandon, *loc. cit.*, p. 36.

32. *Ibid.*

33. *Ibid.*

34. *Ibid.*

35. The Mesquakie, also known as the Fox, purchased their own land in 1854. Hence, they live on a "settlement" rather than a "reservation."

36. Statements to the author.

37. Brandon, *loc. cit.*, p. 37.

38. Robert G. Sherrill, "Red Man's Heritage: The Lagoon of Excrement," *The Nation* (Nov. 10, 1969), p. 501.

39. Brandon, *loc. cit.*, p. 35.

40. Dr. Alan Sorkin, data presented at the hearings before the Subcommittee on Indian Education, *op. cit.*, p. 330.

41. Brightman, "Red Power," p. 37.

42. *Ibid.*

43. *Ibid.*

44. Ralph Nader, "Lo, the Poor Indian," *The New Republic,* March 30, 1968, p. 15. For a detailed analysis of the white colonialism inflicted on the American Indian, see Nader's "American Indians: People Without a Future," *Harvard Law Record,* May 10, 1956, pp. 1–4.

3

The Emerging
Red Educational Renaissance

Indians have become very aware that they, collectively, can materially transfigure their own lives for the better. Nationalism has animated the Indian spirit. Many express a keen awareness of the nationalist revolutions of Asia and Africa and the American civil rights movement. It is as if, under the impact of the international and national revolutions of rising expectations, tribal nationalisms, long submerged, have finally surfaced after a long sleep. The catalyst for the new Indian nationalism resides in renewed hope, a catharsis of fatalism and alienation, that has impelled the red man into politics. And it is through political activism that the native American has begun to exercise a voice in educational decision-making.

Self-reliant Indians have endeavored to transform their schools on a number of occasions. Perhaps the most important Indian-administered educational institution is the Navajos' Rough Rock Demonstration School.[1] Other manifestations of Red Power include the Mesquakies' struggle to win control of their own school near Tama, Iowa, and, of course, the demand of the United Indians of All Tribes on Alcatraz Island for an Indian educational and cultural center. These types of educational expressions of Red Power will undoubtedly proliferate. Indian school board membership, attendance at P.T.A. meetings, and entry into the teaching profession, for example, should increase markedly.

In contrast to a white-administered, culturally biased educational system, a genuinely Indian educational milieu generates high Indian pupil achievement and self-respect. When Indians participate in educational decision-making, they attain to high standards in terms of their own identity and experiential background. They define learning by devising experiences and inquiries that allow their young to legitimate their ancient culture within modern society but simultaneously fulfill the skill requirements exacted by the society for productive employment.

There are some outstanding examples of Red Power at work within educational contexts. The most famous is the Rough Rock experiment, located at Chinle, Arizona.[2] The seven-member school board, entirely Navajo, administers a school that reveres the Indian culture and life-style and teaches occupational skills requisite to a career in the sophisticated American technocracy. So successful has the Rough Rock fusion of ancient and modern worlds been that about twelve thousand visitors, many from overseas, visit annually.

Rough Rock qualifies as a thoroughly Navajo school. Navajo culture, history, and language constitute the major components of the culturally focused core curriculum. Sixty-two of eighty-two full-time employees are Navajo. The school's Cultural Identification Center provides facilities for Navajo writers and artists. Counselors regularly play recordings of Navajo music and rituals in the

dormitories. Teachers encourage the children to encoun-
ter themselves aesthetically and culturally as Navajos.
They establish ties to the community by periodically
visiting pupils' homes to counsel with parents concerning
their children. Parents even live in the dormitories for
two-month periods, serving as paid dormitory aides.
They console children terrified by nightmares and tell
bedtime Navajo folktales. The children are privileged to
travel home on weekends. The school provides transportation. The Rough Rock model demonstrates that the
involvement of the Indian community is a *sine qua non*
for an apposite Indian educational experience. The
resurrection of tribalism is both sufficient and necessary
for genuinely Indian education.

Rough Rock is the most noteworthy, current example
of success in Indian education, but it is not the only one.
The Pima Indians have similarly asserted themselves in
their schools. An all-Indian school board governs a
former BIA school on the Gila River Pima Indian Reservation in Arizona.[3] Navajo parents and students at the
Lukachukai Boarding School have succeeded in sharing
power with the school in matters of curriculum and
governance.[4] There are a few other examples that could
be cited to demonstrate further that Indian involvement
in educational decision-making is growing.

The fact of the matter is that the great majority of Indians find it no longer acceptable to acquiesce to paternalism or stoically endure privation. They seem to have
abruptly denied the fatalism that has until now led them
to accept their plight. They seem increasingly inclined to
turn their anger outward into activism, cultural and
political, rather than inward into apathy, suicide, and
alcoholism. They are very much looking for their own

Selmas.[5] This is their attitudinal revolution: the un-
leashing of a flood tide of frustration that is extremely
difficult to stem with paternalism once in motion. Indian
leaders have become seriously politically active in the
National Congress of American Indians, founded in 1944,
and local and regional groups, such as Indians United
for Survival in Nisqually, Washington, Coalition of
American Indian Citizens in Denver, and United Native
Americans in San Francisco. The delegates of forty tribes
convened at Princeton University on March 25, 1970, to
discuss ways to mobilize Indian political power to improve their condition. They called for militancy in the
pursuit of Indian advancement. This is the ethos that is
alive in the Indian community.

The Indians believe they very much need a post-high
school institution totally committed to Indian needs.[6]
Some activists want an institution resembling Negro
"freedom schools" or Howard University. They aspire to
train Indians for authentic tribal leadership rather than
mere "Uncle Tomahawk" (the Indian equivalent of
"Uncle Tom") accommodation. They hope that, through
the cultivation of Indian leadership, the entire Indian
community can advance as a group rather than regress
as its most promising young people are siphoned off into
Anglo-American society. They feel Indian-controlled
elementary and high schools, colleges, and universities
could educate an emancipated, thoroughly Indian elite
and help students develop a pride in their native American heritage. They claim that the present policy of send-
ing young people to white schools denigrates Indian
dignity and the capacity for self-sufficiency, and that too
many of the best Indians have been co-opted in this
way, induced into a bicultural life, a limbo "between

two cultures," as the anthropologists have popularly explained it. Many young Indians believe that intrinsically Indian education presents the most powerful antidote to the inferiority complex and insecurity that plague the Indian. Indian education, they maintain, produces graduates who advocate unrelentingly that Indian culture is sacred and worth preserving.

The fount of the contemporary Red Power Movement traces to the group of young Indian activists educated in the universities after World War II and Korea. The Indian draftees experienced the modern world of the white man in those wars; they wanted to learn more about that world when they returned from overseas and how they might fit into it. Some of the most inquisitive attended college under the GI Bill. The number of Indian youth attending college for one year or more rose from 6,500 to 17,000 in the decade 1950 to 1960. The number of Navajo students alone rose from a mere three dozen annually immediately after World War II to more than 400 in the early '60s. The Indian collegians learned much about the nontribal world but also soon knew that their place in that world was at best marginal, that the white man's way was not sufficient for them. This disquieting discovery impelled the young Indian intelligentsia to aim at self-determination in education and other realms rather than full-fledged assimilation. They sought, in short, to forge a liberating pluralism for themselves. University education functioned, thus, as the formal course work following the abrupt and involuntary matriculation into white values achieved in the barracks. It was as much alienating as it was informative.[7]

The Indians began to organize politically in the postwar era. They worked assiduously through the National

Congress of American Indians and the National Education Conference.[8] They have more recently organized at regional, local, and tribal levels.[9] The most important organization among college-enrolled Indians is the National Indian Youth Council.[10] The NIYC, founded in 1961, has earned a reputation as the SNCC of Indian affairs.[11] The entire panoply of Indian politics has unquestionably shattered the myth of the silent and vanishing Indian and done much to convert Indian alienation into effective participation.

The Indians no longer rely on evoking liberal guilt feelings to stimulate reform. They now maintain that change will come only through united Indian involvement in the political process. The program of the California Indian Education Association and United Native Americans is exemplary. They have built a substantial grass-roots movement that is having a considerable impact on the schools. The consequence is that Indian citizens now help to develop and select curricula, serve on school boards, and administer and control teacher training programs. They are ensuring that the schools will teach Indian history and culture and hire Indian teachers, resource people, and teacher aides. Don Wanatee, secretary of the recalcitrant Mesquakie Tribe of Iowa, expresses the pan-tribal national mood aptly, "I think it is time that the Indian people throughout the United States are given the right to choose what their children should learn and must learn in order to preserve their tribal ways." [12] Mr. Wanatee and his fellow Indians do not particularly seek confrontation with white America in articulating this desire. They realize that their most significant struggle inheres not in inflammatory resistance but the intellectual re-creation of a vibrant tribalism that will eventually transform federal policy. However, they remain capable of warlike militancy, as a final resource, should cautious Red Power fail.

Indian political activism most significantly embraces increasing participation in educational decisions. Political power and educational self-determination are merely opposite sides of the same coin. For example, the Rough Rock Demonstration School reflects pan-Indian consciousness surfacing at a specific, historical juncture after having been long submerged. The Indians, inspired by their new political awareness, have imagined community control of their schools and an intertribal educational center to preserve and transmit their historic tradition. But the Indian, lacking detectable political power until now, has been unable to control the education of his own children. He has consequently gravitated to the brink of cultural extinction. His recent vigilance springs from a disconcerting realization that he must now mobilize every vestige of power to provide for his cultural continuity. He intuits the ineluctable reality that Red Power and educational renaissance are both requisite to the regeneration of Indian culture.[13]

NOTES

1. See Paul Conklin, "Good Day at Rough Rock: Navajo Demonstration School," *American Education* (February, 1967), pp. 4–9. See also "Participation of Indians in Public Life," *Navajo Times*, Window Rock, Arizona, Feb. 2, 1967, and "Pride of the Reservation: Rough Rock Demonstration School Is Working Model for Indian Community College," *Time*, April 11, 1969, p. 67.

2. Personal observations and interviews, Rough Rock School, Chinle, Arizona, June 26, 28, and 29, 1970.

3. Personal observation, Gila River Pima Indian School.

4. Interviews, Lukachukai Boarding School.

5. Among the books that deal most competently with the new Indian activism are Vine Deloria, Jr., *Custer Died for Your Sins* (The Macmillan Company, 1969); Edgar Cahn (ed.), *Our Brother's Keeper* (The World Publishing Company, 1969); and Stan Steiner, *The New Indians* (Harper & Row, Publishers, Inc., 1968).

6. An important Indian leader, Jack D. Forbes, professor of anthropology at the University of California, has argued for a culturally expressive university as the Indians' only hope for survival: "Most native Americans of tribal affiliation wish to preserve their identity both as 'Indians' and as members of a specific tribe. In the long run this probably cannot be done without tribally-controlled schools and an inter-tribal university. The experience of our nationalities and groups throughout the world would seem to prove that a people must possess a cultural, educational and intellectual center of its own in order to survive and advance. If Tribal Americans are to preserve their identity, an intertribal, native-controlled university would seem to be a necessity." ("An American Indian University: A Proposal for Survival," *Journal of American Indian Education,* Vol. V, January, 1966, pp. 1–2.)

7. Stan Steiner, *The New Indians* (Harper & Row, Publishers, Inc., 1968), p. 31.

8. See, for example, Wendell Chino, *Challenge of Changing Winds,* keynote address, National Congress of American Indians, Washington, D.C., November, 1966; "The Custer Myth Revised," The National Congress of American Indians' *Sentinel,* Convention Issue, Vol. XI, No. 1 (Fall, 1966); "Declaration of Indian Purpose," American Indian Chicago Conference, June, 1961; "First Convention of the National Congress of American Indians: Proceedings," Nov. 15, 1944, 55 pp. (mimeographed); *Policy Resolutions of the National Conference of American Indians: 1954–1966* (Washington,

D.C.: NCAI, 1967), 131 pp.; and Oliver La Farge, "The Indians Want a New Frontier," *The New York Times Magazine*, June 11, 1961.

9. The Indians have organized such groups as the Native American Committee (Chicago), American Indian Movement (Minneapolis), and the American Indian Information and Action Group (Milwaukee). The Pit River Indian Council even mobilized in June of 1970 an invasion to reclaim 3.5 million acres of their historic tribal lands in Northern California. A party of 150 St. Regis Mohawk Indians seized and claimed title to Loon and Stanley Islands in the St. Lawrence River on May 9, 1970. These are but a few examples of the organization and activism at regional, local, and tribal levels.

10. *Indian Affairs*, the newsletter of the Association on American Indian Affairs, occasionally reports the activities of the National Indian Youth Council. The Council also publishes its own journal, *Americans Before Columbus*, which reflects more precisely the mood and intent of the young Indian activists. One may subscribe to *Americans Before Columbus* by remitting $5 to the National Indian Youth Council, P.O. Box 118, Schurz, Nev. 89427. The address for *Indian Affairs* is 432 Park Avenue South, New York, N.Y. 10016.

11. Excellent expressions of the National Indian Youth Council philosophy, one by a white jurist, include Clyde Warrior, "How Should an Indian Act?" *Americans Before Columbus*, Vol. II, No. 5 (June, 1965); Felix S. Cohen, "Indian Self-Government," *Americans Before Columbus*, Vol. II, No. 5 (June, 1965); and Clyde Warrior, "Which One Are You? Five Types of Young Indians," *Americans Before Columbus*, Vol. II, No. 4 (December, 1964).

12. Interview with Don Wanatee, secretary, Mesquakie Tribal Council, Box #40, R. R. #2, Tama, Iowa, June 3, 1970.

13. For an elaboration of the relationship between Indian

activism and educational decision-making, see the longer version of G. Louis Heath's "The Life and Education of the American Indian," *Illinois Quarterly*, Vol. 33, No. 3 (February, 1971), pp. 16–38, reprinted in this book in edited form. Also, see Estelle Fuchs, "American Indian Education: Time to Redeem an Old Promise," *Saturday Review* (Jan. 24, 1970), pp. 54–57 and 74–75.

II
BROWN DEMANDS
FOR BETTER EDUCATION

The problems that the Chicanos in the United States face are considerable. In the cities, they suffer the physical and spiritual insults that ghetto life inflicts. On the farms, they pick seasonal crops for low wages under appalling conditions. Recently, a political education movement has allowed brown citizens to become aware of the injustice of their plight. The Chicanos have begun to demand that the institutions of this society, including the schools, serve their desperate needs.

The most outstanding Mexican-American leader is Cesar Chavez. He, more than any other individual, launched the political education campaign that journalists now call the Brown Power Movement or La Raza. His impoverished early life and struggle to organize the United Farm Workers Organizing Committee exemplify the educational, employment, and even ecological and psychic problems the Chicanos must resolve.

4

Cesar Chavez and the United Farm Workers Organizing Committee*

Cesar Chavez's National Farm Workers Union is a dualistic movement: it embodies both social and religious components. It is, of course, socially, a union movement focused upon the right to collective bargaining. It is also a religious movement because the membership is virtually totally Catholic and they regard their leader, Cesar Chavez, as a secular saint, the personalized spearhead of the Chicano millennium.[1] Pope John has even conferred his blessing upon Chavez's union: "We for that matter express our satisfaction with those sons of ours throughout the whole world who actively are engaged in the movement of agricultural workers with the intention of elevating the economic and social level of the communities of agricultural workers."[2] The infusion of religious fervor into the movement has impelled it far beyond bread-and-butter unionism. Chavez's belief that he has a special mission to fulfill, plus the papal approbation, has solidly fused the secular and theological. The result has been a very dynamic and en-

* Originally appeared in *Interracial Review*, Summer, 1971. Reprinted by permission.

during form of agrarian unionism, built in spite of fantastic adversity and a paucity of resources.

A Note on the Church

Although the Catholic Church is now firmly committed to support Chavez's union, such was not always the case. When Chavez first began to mobilize his union, he ran into a wall of indifference on the part of the church. Chavez wrote about what he regarded as a callous separation of his church and social problems:

> It was not until some of us moved to Delano and began working to build the National Farm Workers Association that we really saw how far removed from the people the parish church was. In fact, we could not get any help at all from the priests of Delano. When the strike began, they told us we could not even use the church's auditorium for the meetings. The farm workers' money helped build that auditorium! But the Protestants were there again, in the form of the California Migrant Ministry, and they began to help in little ways, here and there.[3]

Chavez argued that it was not only his union's right to appeal to the church, but also its duty. He argued that appealing to the church for guidance and support should be as natural as appealing to government. He praised the church for its humanistic public positions but stressed that it was not proceeding effectively to enact the imperative of brotherly love. He was particularly quick to point out the difference between benevolent paternalism and serious organization:

The Catholic Charities of the Catholic Church has millions of dollars earmarked for the poor. But often the money is spent for food baskets for the needy instead of for effective action to eradicate the causes of poverty. The men and women who administer this money sincerely want to help their brothers. It should be our duty to help direct the attention to the basic needs of the Mexican-Americans in our society . . . needs which cannot be satisfied with baskets of food, but rather with effective organizing at the grass-roots level.[4]

Chavez and the Chicano workers appealed successfully to the moral sensibilities of the church. For example, many priests and nuns were in Sacramento, California, during the spring of 1965 for nonviolent demonstrations in support of Chavez's union.[5] Their involvement has continued and deepened. Church members have also evinced considerable sympathy and provided substantial support for the vineyard workers. Chavez's appeal was certainly neither misdirected nor wasted. As the leader of a contingent of impoverished, oppressed Catholic workers, he knew that the church would have to revert to medievalism in order to ignore completely the workers' plight. The modern church proved incapable of that; it eventually conceded the merit of Chavez's petition for social relevance.

CHAVEZ'S LIFE, PHILOSOPHY, AND ACTIVISM [6]

Cesar Chavez's gravitation to union organization stems logically from his impoverished childhood. There was no sudden vision or union workshop on the needs of the poor for him. He spent his first ten austere years on his father's depressed farm in Yuma, Arizona. The Chavez family was forced to begin a migrant life when they lost their few sparse acres. They moved continually from town to town and from migrant camp to migrant camp. Cesar often helped his parents obtain a livelihood by fishing in irrigation ditches and picking mustard greens and weed. He recalls having attended over thirty schools by the eighth grade. He never attended high school as it became a survival imperative that he drop out of school to work in the fields. The Chavez family finally settled, after much wandering, in the most execrable of the barrios in San Jose, California. The barrio offered the deprivation and bleak living conditions to match its name, *Sal Si Puedes*—"Get Out If You Can."

Cesar's father served as a living example of a union organizer to the young Chavez. The elder Chavez became an organizer in 1939. Cesar recollects:

> One of the old CIO unions began organizing workers in the dried-fruit industry, so my father and my uncle became members. Sometimes the men would meet at our house, and I remember seeing their picket signs and hearing them talk. They had a strike and my father and uncle picketed at night. It made a deep impression on me. . . . From that time on my father joined every agricultural union that came along. Often he was the first one to join, and when I was nineteen, I joined the National Agricultural Workers' Union.[7]

Unfortunately, every strike Cesar's father participated in failed. Cesar learned intimately the tactical and ideological blunders to avoid.

Father Donald McDonnell played a significant role in Cesar's intellectual development. Father McDonnell, a very erudite man, had a zeal for labor history and a compassion for the *campesinos* in the fields. He and Cesar often discussed doctrines of social justice and the encyclicals of the popes. Cesar recalls, "I began going to the bracero camps with him to help with Mass; to the city jail with him to talk to the prisoners—anything to be with him so that he could tell me more about the farm labor movement." Father McDonnell certainly contributed substantially to the nurture of Chavez's social consciousness and concern for the oppressed.

Cesar Chavez was picking apricots and peaches in the fields near San Jose when Fred Ross, a representative for the Community Service Organization (CSO), enlisted him as a community organizer. For ten years Chavez organized farm workers throughout California. He eventually became director of the National CSO. He left, however, disgusted with the staid, middle-class strategies of his colleagues, in order to organize a grass-roots union of farm workers. He complained that the semi-professional and professional officers of the CSO could not communicate with the workers whom they hoped to help. Chavez examines his revulsion: "I personally felt pained to see how little trust they had in the people." Thus, Cesar Chavez renounced elitist paternalism for democratic action.

Cesar Chavez founded an effective National Farm Workers Union. He owes his success to the respect of the Mexican workers that he enjoys. He possesses a genuine and abiding faith in his people. The workers know this faith is unshakable; Chavez's tribulations have earned their trust. They vest Chavez with a virtually sacrosanct legitimacy that has enabled him to lead a poorly funded, frail movement to internationally renowned victory over powerful California agribusiness. Chavez eschews paternalism and professionalism in favor of the ancient principle that only the people know what is good for themselves. He feels that he is simply one of the farm workers who has a special mission to introduce coherence and sting into a militant strain of agrarian populism. Chavez is an authentic exponent of the communal democracy of the barrio and the ageless *campesino* suspicion of the *gobierno,* the leader. Hence, he insists on living on the same five-dollar allowance as everyone else working for the union. His ability to lead and still participate has been the critical factor in the adept organizing of a union under what were objectively very inauspicious conditions.

Cesar Chavez fervently espouses the ideology and tactics of nonviolence. He has studied the writings and lives of Gandhi and Zapata and learned community action strategy from Saul Alinsky. His goal is reform through nonviolent organization. He shuns violence, even in response to the acts of brutality his movement has suffered, as being ultimately divisive and destructive to those who resort to it. Chavez maintains that violence will destroy the very possibility of the mutual trust absolutely necessary for lasting social change. He emphasizes cooperation, equal rights, and nonviolence as a means to long-term improvements and survival for all. Although his union is composed basically of Chicano, Catholic workers, this is so only because most vineyard workers happen to have these socially distinguishing characteristics. Chavez feels that an intentionally, racially exclusive movement translates into violent action that can, at best, only secure short-term gains. He accordingly opened his union to everyone, irrespective of ethnic, racial, and religious background. He knows that only a movement that brings together all types of poor people will be effective in winning industry-wide battles as well as promising larger sociostructural change.

Chavez concurs with Gandhi's admonition that a leader of the poor should live as the poor. Only in this way will the leader retain his sense of oneness with the oppressed and his resoluteness of purpose. Otherwise, despite himself, he may exploit his position. Accordingly, Chavez's family lives in unmistakable poverty. His wife and eight children occupy a modest, two-bedroom, frame home in the Delano barrio. This qualifies eminently as self-denial when one contrasts Chavez's deprivation with the privilege and affluence of other American union officials. Sacrifice is the basic parameter of his life. He maintains that leaders should suffer for the poor who are satiated with pain. Chavez philosophizes: "The poor have the biggest stake in peace. But they are the ones who can do the least because they are so busy scratching out a living to get something to eat." For Cesar Chavez, self-abnegation is the foremost prerequisite for effective leadership.

Chavez began a fast in the spring of 1968 that lasted twenty-five days. He sacrificed one fifth of his body weight, thirty-five pounds, to "the pain and suffering of the farm workers." He ingested nothing save water and an occasional few ounces of bouillon and unsweetened grapefruit juice. He became so weak he could hardly move. On the twenty-fifth day of his fast, Cesar Chavez broke bread with the late Senator Robert F. Kennedy, who had flown to Delano to be with the Chicano leader. Senator Kennedy commended Chavez's fast as a personal expression to the world that "violence is no answer." An assassin's bullet felled the senator three months later, just after he had claimed victory in California's presidential primary. His margin of victory had been the Chicano vote.

Cesar Chavez fervidly believes in personalizing social change. He insists that only through the drudgery of contacting and informing people on a face-to-face basis can significant and enduring reform be achieved. In short, only through grass-roots education and participation can the *status quo* be altered beneficially, of, by, and for the people. Chavez relates: "I was going around the country for a long time giving speeches, but I've learned now that the real thing is to be on the picket line. But you've got to talk to the people, knock on every damn door, make the pitch and play the percentages." Chavez's equation for social equity and justice is based upon people. The product of that equation is that individuals suffering deprivation and discrimination are entitled to certain fundamental human rights and civilized employment conditions.

LA HUELGA, THE STRIKE

The farm workers union's strike, La Huelga, began September 16, 1965, the day of Mexican independence. On that day, Chavez's National Farm Workers of America (NFWA) voted to support Filipino labor leader Larry Itliong's Agricultural Workers Organizing Committee (AWOC) in a walkout against DiGiorgio Fruit Corporation and Schenley Industries, Inc. Itliong soon became Chavez's chief lieutenant, a status he has since continuously possessed. NFWA and AWOC eventually voted to merge into a strengthened United Farm

Workers Organizing Committee (UFWOC) in order to deal more adequately with the hostile opposition, even from the ranks of other unions. The Teamsters Union, for example, actually favored the continuance of braceroism (importing Mexican nationals for seasonal harvesting) and even signed a "sweetheart" contract with one of the major growers. The late Walter Reuther and his United Auto Workers have been the major exceptions to the unconcern and antipathy of big labor. Reuther pledged $5,000 monthly to Chavez's union until the strike succeeded. But the bulk of bureaucratically encrusted and benefit-fattened labor has proved insensitive.

The consumer action arm of the strike has been the boycott. Chavez appealed to imbibers of the crushed grape to refuse to purchase wine produced by companies using nonunion grapes. The wineries that bottled wine under their own names collapsed first under the cyclonic impact of the consumer boycott. They were the most easily identifiable targets. Perilli-Minetti folded, followed by Gallo, Almaden, and Christian Brothers. Paul Masson signed with Chavez in September, 1968, bringing into the fold one of the few remaining nationally advertised wineries. Chavez then began to pressure seriously the table grape growers who are less subject to immediate threat because they do not market under their own names. The first two large table grape growers to sign were Bruno Dispoto and the Bianco Brothers, who together cultivate more than 3,000 acres of vineyards in Kern, Tulare, and Riverside counties and employ 1500 workers each. Their initial contracts provided a minimum wage of $1.75 an hour plus 25 cents a box of grapes picked. Employers paid another 12 cents an hour into health and welfare benefit funds over the entire contract period. The National Conference of Catholic Bishops, under the auspices of the Federal Mediation and Conciliation Service, negotiated the contracts. By July, 1970, Chavez had reached an accord with twenty-six growers in the Kern and Tulare County region who produce one half of the table grapes grown in California. The growers granted Chavez's principal demands that the United Farm Workers Organizing Committee represent the vineyard workers in bargaining on their wages and working conditions. The agreement also guaranteed a minimum wage of $1.80 an hour plus fringe benefits and limitations on pesticide use. The heavy public demand for union-label grapes had provided the final leverage Chavez needed to compel the growers to recognize his union and agree to an equitable contract.[8]

Compounding the misery of poor living and working conditions, the Chicano field workers have suffered incredibly the growers' use of pesticides. Many have become temporarily blind, often incurring permanent eye damage; others have suffered long periods of nausea and vomiting, and all too frequently died from the long-term effects. Chavez fought unrelentingly for a contract clause that delivered to the union the right to control pesticide spraying. He finally won the clause when the Senate hearings on the topic found Safeway samples of table grapes to contain, as UFWOC had insisted, 18 parts per million of aldrin, a toxic pesticide, at 180 times the FDA minimum tolerance. Dr. Irma West, a principal witness for Chavez's union, testified that one hundred million pounds of pesticides are applied annually without appropriate health safeguards in California agricultural operations. The present UFWOC contracts protect both field worker and consumer. The Chavez contracts guarantee that the delivered produce will contain tolerance or less than tolerance levels of pesticides. Chavez notes with pride that "we are the first union in the United States to have contracts governing pesticides, but there is still a long way to go from here. We have to educate our members to the real dangers of pesticides. Once people realize just what they are and what they do, it'll do more to put a ban on widespread pollution than anything else." Poisoned grapes injure and kill both consumers and workers. It is this ecological imperative which is now linking the consumer protection movement and Chavez's United Farm Workers Organizing Committee.[9]

With his vineyard successes behind him, Chavez has launched or planned major campaigns among growers of melons and other produce in the Imperial Valley and among fruit and vegetable workers in the vast Salinas Valley.[10] The organization of the vineyards is only the prelude to a larger mobilization of a virtually invisible agrarian poor (the superhighways and Holiday Inns offer Middle America no vantage points) to whom the benefits of the industrial revolution, and the panoply of social innovations that went with it, have never been passed. Chavez's incipient social movement, focused on unionism, promises a more equitable distribution of the good things of life. Perhaps the rural poor can finally force their way into the twentieth century.

Cesar Chavez talks about the idea he made a reality:

Movements come and go, student, war and so on, but we hang on. We're five years old now. Fifteen years ago there were only three or four people trying to organize farm workers. We didn't have experience then, just the idea.

We chose Delano because the vines need work

nine months out of the year and the workers are around longer. It was really rough at first. My wife, Helen, worked in the fields while I organized full-time. We starved for a while building the National Farm Workers Association, then five years later created the Union. We couldn't use the word "union" at first because people were frightened by it. They said, "You're crazy; it'll never happen." It's happened.[11]

Chavez has religiously acted out his faith in the Mexican-American field worker. In the crucible of adversity, he has forged a social movement, imbued with religious symbolism, that has given the Chicano worker new hope for a life of material and spiritual integrity in a society that has historically imposed inhuman conditions on powerless, low-status citizens.[12] Cesar Chavez and the United Farm Workers Organizing Committee have enabled impoverished field workers—mostly Chicano due to both systematic discrimination and historic accident—to assert the dignity that belongs, as a principle of both theological doctrine and social justice, to every man.

NOTES

1. For a good presentation and analysis of the movement Cesar Chavez leads, see Peter Matthiessen, *Sal Si Puedes: Cesar Chavez and the New American Revolution* (Random House, Inc., 1970).

2. Quoted in Penfield Jensen, "Knock on Every Door, An Account of the Grape Boycott," *Earth Times,* July, 1970, p. 22.

3. Cesar E. Chavez, "The Mexican-American and the Church," *El Grito,* Vol. 1, No. 4 (Summer, 1968), p. 10.

4. *Ibid.*, p. 12. Cesar Chavez summarizes his thoughts about the church as follows (p. 12): "Finally, in a nutshell, what do we want the church to do? We don't ask for more cathedrals. We don't ask for bigger churches or fine gifts. We ask for its presence with us, beside us, as Christ among us. We ask the church to *sacrifice with the people* for social change, for justice, and for love of brother. We don't ask for words. We ask for deeds. We don't ask for paternalism. We ask for servanthood."

5. Personal observation.

6. This account of Cesar Chavez's life draws heavily upon Penfield Jensen, "Talk to the People . . . A Conversation with Cesar Chavez," and "Knock on Every Door," *Earth Times*, July, 1970; Matthiessen, *op. cit.*; Stan Steiner, *La Raza: The Mexican Americans* (Harper & Row, Publishers, Inc., 1970); John Gregory Dunne, *Delano: The Story of the California Grape Strike* (Farrar, Straus, and Giroux, Inc., 1967); and Peter Matthiessen, "Cesar Chavez, A Profile," *The New Yorker*, June 21 and 28, 1969.

7. Steiner, *op. cit.*, p. 313.

8. Dick Meister, "Grape Growers and Workers Reach Accord," *San Francisco Chronicle*, July 29, 1970, p. 1.

9. See *Pesticides, the Poisons We Eat*, UFWOC, AFL-CIO, Box 130, Delano, Calif. 93215, and Jensen, "Knock on Every Door, An Account of the Grape Boycott," pp. 22–25.

Cesar Chavez and his brother know very well the destructive potential of pesticides. They have experienced them. "My brother and I worked in every fruit you can imagine. This time it was peaches. They had just introduced a new economic poison, that's what they call them, and we were hired to spray during the dormant season up in Santa Clara County.

"The only warning they gave us was 'Don't get any of it in your eyes.' Well, we got into trouble. We both got sick, started vomiting. I began having trouble focusing, began seeing double and so on. I got pretty scared. Fortunately, I had the good sense to see a doctor. It went away shortly thereafter. I still get sick to my stomach even now when I get near those sprays.

"About eight years ago, when the union was very small, and I was doing all the case work, a worker came in saying: 'I don't know what's wrong with me. I can't breathe right and I can't focus. When I look at you I see two people. The further you get away the further apart the two images get.' I asked him if he had been near any pesticides. He didn't even know what they were. It turned out that he was on his third job since he's worked sprays. I couldn't get disability for him because the cause of illness couldn't be traced to any specific employer. He was our first case and Workman's Compensation wouldn't touch it." (Jensen, "Talk to the People," p. 21.)

10. Meister, *loc. cit.*, p. 1.

11. Jensen, "Talk to the People," p. 21.

12. Cesar Chavez's union is only one part, albeit significant, of the national farm worker-Chicano assertion of collective power. The author regards the following works to be the most important ones on the movement and the conditions from which it flows:

> *Basta!* (*Enough*) *The Tale of Our Struggle.* Farm Worker Press, Inc., 1966.
>
> Citizens' Board of Inquiry Into Hunger and Malnutrition in the United States, *Hunger, U.S.A.* Beacon Press, Inc., 1968.
>
> Dunne, John Gregory, *Delano: The Story of the California Grape Strike.* Farrar, Straus and Giroux, Inc., 1967.
>
> Galarza, Ernesto, *Merchants of Labor: The Mexican Bracero Story.* McNally & Loftin, Inc., 1964.
>
> ———— *Strangers in Our Fields.* Joint U.S.–Mexico Trade Union Committee, U.S. Section, Washington, D.C., 1956.
>
> Grebler, Leo, *The Schooling Gap: Signs of Progress.*

Mexican-American Study Project, University of California at Los Angeles, 1967.

Inter-Agency Committee on Mexican-American Affairs, *The Mexican American: A New Focus on Opportunity*. Testimony Presented at the Cabinet Committee Hearings on Mexican-American Affairs, El Paso, Texas, Oct. 26–28, 1967. Washington, D.C., n.d.

Madsen, William, *The Mexican-Americans of South Texas*. Holt, Rinehart and Winston, Inc., 1964.

Nabokov, Peter, *Tijerina and the Courthouse Raid*. University of New Mexico Press, 1969.

National Education Association—Department of Rural Education, *The Invisible Minority: Pero No Vencibles*. National Education Association, 1966.

Nelson, Eugene, *Huelga: The First Hundred Days of the Great Delano Grape Strike*. Farm Worker Press, Inc., 1966.

Rubel, Arthur J., *Across the Tracks: Mexican-Americans in a Texas City*. University of Texas Press, 1966.

Salinas, José Lazaro, *La Emigración de Braceros*. Mexico City: "Cauh Temoc," 1955.

Samora, Julian (ed.), *La Raza: Forgotten Americans*. University of Notre Dame Press, 1966.

Turner, William, "No Dice for Braceros," *Ramparts*, September, 1965, pp. 14–16.

"We Are Not Alone," *El Grito del Norte*, Vol. II, No. 5 (March 28, 1969), p. 5.

5
Compulsory Mis-Education
for the Chicano

The educational process is none too successful for
Mexican-Americans. The statistics empirically corroborate this inference. The data gathered by the U.S. Office
of Education's National Advisory Committee on Mexican-American Education provide the details about the
two million Chicanos of school age:

> The drop-out rate in Texas for Chicano high
> school youth is 89%. In California 50% of Chicano
> high school students drop out between the 10th
> and 11th grades.
> In the Southwest the average Chicano child at-
> tains to only a seventh grade education.
> In Texas' Rio Grande Valley region 80% of the
> Chicano children are two years behind the achieve-
> ment level of their white classmates by the fifth
> grade. As for adults, 44.3% of the barrio residents
> are "functionally illiterate" and 20% never at-
> tended school "at all."
> Almost no Chicanos attend college. For example,
> less than one-half of one per cent of college stu-
> dents at the seven campuses of the University of
> California are Chicanos. This constitutes a remark-
> able underrepresentation in a state where 14% of

the public school students are Mexican-Americans. And finally, the median level of education among Mexican-Americans is 8.6 years of school.[1]

The appalling assumption of public school teachers and administrators is that Chicano learners should be decultured. In fact, their attitudes are very similar to those frontiersman, assimilationist values described in the section on Indians. As with the Indians, the schools are operating with the intent of eliminating—at least subduing—the parent language and culture. No wonder the data above are as they are. Since putative "educative" experiences are, in fact, really structured to deny the authority of the Chicano language and culture, it is logical that psychologically healthy Chicano students will attempt to escape the school system. To remain in school and seriously attempt to learn within the Anglo-contrived learning environment is to suffer, as the Indian, a virulent form of hyperalienation.[2] No school system can claim that this outcome is a legitimate learning objective.

The crossover phenomenon that typifies the Indian's school learning achievement is also true for the Chicano. Mexican-American and Anglo children begin school at about the same measured achievement level. But the Chicano children lose ground to the Anglo children as they progress through the white-oriented curriculum and are subjected to culturally biased teacher behavior. As time passes, the dropout (really the push-out) rate increases dramatically. When high school graduation arrives only the Chicanos who are no longer Chicanos pick up a diploma. In fact, the only junctures at which Chicanos and Anglos achieve commensurably are in kindergarten and in the senior year of high school. At age five, the Chicano child still believes in his home culture and the alleged altruistic intentions of the school. And at graduation the achievement levels are equal because the Chicanos who have made the psychological transition to being white or managed the incredibly difficult task of emulating Anglo behavior and values for thirteen years are the only brown students still in school. Thus, the school gets defined as a success through a combination of attrition and assimilation.[3]

Chicano students tend to be tracked into nonacademic curricula, where skills, not thinking, are taught, due to, among other factors, the bias of I.Q. tests. The tests generally utilized in the public schools are biased toward Anglo culture and life; they do not objectively, fully measure capacity for learning. Since the tests tap largely the learning of culture, and the culture tested is white, it is not logically inconsistent that Chicano students perform very poorly on the examinations. Only the highly assimilated Chicanos will do well. The real Chicano, like the real Indian, is a failure by virtue of the very fact he is a Chicano. Indian leader Jack Forbes calls this process "mental genocide."[4] Perhaps the term is more than pejorative.

The psychologists in the schools play a considerable role in the processing of Chicano students into the low-status, dead-end tracks. Thomas Carter reports a telling contrast in the impact of school psychologists' decisions upon the lives of Chicano children. One psychologist was Anglo and the other was Spanish-speaking. They were testing, with standard instruments, to determine which children should be placed in special education classes. The white psychologist recommended that 75 percent be assigned to the special education classes. The Spanish-speaking psychologist recommended that only 26 percent be so placed.[5] Since the standard psychometric instruments do not measure Chicano children's intelligence validly, the test examiner's attitudes become a crucial consideration in the assignment of Chicano youngsters to special education classes and other low tracks. Thus, it is very important that Chicano psychologists—at least psychologists studied in Chicano culture—administer intelligence and achievement tests to Chicano learners.

The treatment the Chicano child has received in the schools has not been completely nonviolent. A sizable number of schools in the Southwest condone the beating of Mexican-American children who are so bold as to speak Spanish. During the classroom lessons, teachers habitually intimidate Chicano children who speak Spanish. They rigidly enforce "no Spanish" rules and assert that it is impolite to speak Spanish, often largely because they speak no second language themselves. They are very much inspired by the philosophy of assimilate or drop out. The assault upon the last major vestige of a culture, the spoken language, is a form of psychological violence that far exceeds the damage of regular paddlings and strappings. It is implicit (if not, in fact, official) public school policy.[6] This psychologically barbarous deculturization is merely an extension of the cultural liquidation that began with the colonization of the region and its eventual integration into the American empire. It is certain that "Manifest Destiny" still thrives in the schools of the Southwest.

Dennis H. Mangers, former principal of the Earlimart School District's elementary school in California, attempted to meet the actual needs of Chicano pupils but was fired for his efforts. He describes some of the conditions he attempted to reform as follows:

The law required that the school district provide Class A lunches for children whose parents had no work and could not afford to pay. I soon noticed that very few youngsters ever received the benefit of a free lunch due to some rather elaborate criteria that successfully precluded most of them from qualifying. It seemed very strange to me that so many of our children announced daily that they were going home for lunch and then would reappear on the playground just five minutes later. In investigating further, I found that a great number of the children simply could not stand the embarrassment of being made to go through the lunch line when they had no money and could not qualify for a free lunch. Their ploy, then, was to say they were going home for lunch even though they knew very well there was no food at home and they would be back on the grounds in minutes, hungrier than ever.

Among those who did manage to eat in the cafeteria, I noticed many children having difficulty eating some of the food prepared by the exclusively Anglo staff of cooks. In questioning the children and many of their parents, I found that for years they had been asking if rice and beans could be substituted for mashed potatoes occasionally. When we called in a state consultant, she told us that since rice and beans were surplus commodities and available in huge quantities, there should be no problem. Furthermore, she provided our cooks with many Mexican-style recipes that were simple and economical.

The school board, however, soon got wind of the

consultant's suggestions through a disgruntled cook, and in a meeting of unparalleled vitriol, one member lost his temper and said, "If these damn Mexican kids are too good for American food, then ship the little bastards back to Tiajuana."

The inevitable finally occurred. The school board had subverted the intent of the laws so openly that the state was obliged to cut the district off the surplus commodity program. When notified of the state's decision, the board was elated. Now they didn't even have to pretend to give free lunches. Since no big money was involved, just surplus rice and beans for hungry children, they callously let the program collapse.

Because the growers on the board accept huge subsidies from the Government for letting land lie idle, it is impossible to comprehend how they can resent hungry Mexican-American children getting a small subsidy for food unless you understand their ultimate aim: to preserve an abundance of cheap labor.

When proposing new programs to the board, I prepared meticulously but always found the reaction the same. After many a stormy board meeting, we discovered that proposed changes had been approved only because of the board's desire to get their hands on large amounts of federal money. Their hope was, of course, that later they could quietly divert the funds into the "regular district program" and cut their own tax rate.

Because of these funds, we were able to start a preschool for three- and four-year-olds, and move from two three-hour kindergarten sessions to four all-day sessions. A talented young Mexican-American teacher was brought from New Mexico to open "English as a Second Language" classes. We began having Spanish lessons for a small group of teachers and met three mornings a week before school.

The P.T.A. meetings, always poorly attended and totally dominated by the growers' wives, actually saw an increase in attendance from the Mexican-American community for a short time as word was passed that the new principal was involving their children more than ever before. As no Spanish translation of the program was ever allowed, however, interest soon waned again.

The one change most vitally needed, but unfortunately the most sacrosanct of all the sacred cows, had to do with the reading program.

A reading levels program had been devised nearly ten years before when the number of Mexican-American enrollments began to rise. Through a levels testing program, children were placed in classes homogeneously on the basis of scores. The result, of course, was that growers' children were segregated into top "enrichment" groups while non-English-speaking Mexican children were lumped into "remedial" groups with other children of low I.Q. as measured by standardized tests. The levels system was inviolate; I couldn't crack it. The teachers who were considered the "best" of the returning crop were always assigned to the top groups as reward for signing on for another year. The lowest groups went to those least equipped to help them.[7]

The full picture of the Chicano child's situation in the schools is depressing. He encounters preposterous handicaps from the very first day of school. The language used in the classroom is English. Yet he speaks no or very little English. He comes from a father-dominated home, but the elementary classroom is female-dominated.

The middle-class, white values that inspire the class-room culture are a bewilderment to him. He has never heard or seen anything like it in his impoverished environment. His keen sense of discomfort does not produce high achievement. It is more likely to produce withdrawal or flight.[8]

California's curriculum for the "migrant schools" exemplifies the cultural bleaching to which the Anglo educational establishment is myopically committed. For example, the curriculum offers the migrant children:

> Physical education—English cultural games and activities
> Creative arts and crafts—Introduction to English culture, music and song
> Arithmetic—Concrete objects, English concept of arithmetic
> Social Studies—Developing knowledge of characteristics of English culture [9]

This curriculum is extremely monochromatic, virtually guaranteeing identity crises among sensitive Chicano children. The Chicano learner who is initially unaware that he is supposed to be "culturally disadvantaged" might wonder at the heavy doses of white culture. He eventually learns the embittering fact that schools and teachers regard him as rather barbaric and uncivilized.

NOTES

1. Data reported in Stan Steiner, *La Raza: The Mexican Americans* (Harper & Row, Publishers, Inc., 1969), p. 215.
2. The tragic impact of the Anglo curriculum upon the Chicano learner is summarized in the booklet *The Mexican*

American: Quest for Equality (U.S. Office of Education, 1968).

3. Leo Grebler's *The Schooling Gap: Signs of Progress* (Mexican-American Study Project, University of California at Los Angeles, 1967) surveys the effects of educational regression among Chicanos.

4. See Lehman L. Brightman, "Mental Genocide: Some Notes on Federal Boarding Schools for Indians," *Inequality in Education*, No. 7, Feb. 10, 1971 (Harvard Center for Law and Education), pp. 15–19.

5. Thomas P. Carter, *Mexican Americans in School: A History of Educational Neglect* (Teachers College, Columbia University, 1970). See also Pablo Roca, "Problems of Adapting Intelligence Scales from One Culture to Another," *High School Journal*, January, 1955, pp. 124–131, and Thomas R. Garth and Johnson D. Harper, "The Intelligence and Achievement of Mexican Children in the U.S.," *Journal of Abnormal Social Psychology*, July–Sept., 1934, pp. 222–229.

6. See these excellent references:

    Holland, William R., "Language Barrier as an Educational Problem of Spanish-Speaking Children," *Exceptional Children*, Sept., 1960, pp. 42–50.

    Masella, Aristide B., "Help for Newly-Arrived Spanish-Speaking Students," *High Points*, December, 1966, pp. 64–67.

    Mendez, Aida, and Lee, Caroline (eds.), *Trends Conference on Education of the Mexican American in San Diego County*, San Diego University, May 13, 1967. San Diego City Schools, 1968.

    New Mexico State Conference on Education of the Disadvantaged, 1966, *Report of Proceedings*. Santa Fe: New Mexico State Department of Education, 1966.

    Palomares, Uvaldo H., and Cummuns, Emery J., *Assessment of Rural Mexican-American Pupils in Preschool and Grades One Through Six, Preliminary Report.*

Sacramento: California State Department of Education, 1967.

7. Dennis H. Mangers, "Education in the Grapes of Wrath," *The National Elementary Principal*, Vol. L, No. 2 (November, 1970), pp. 38–40. Copyright 1970, National Association of Elementary School Principals, NEA. All rights reserved. Reprinted by permission.

8. See John Plakos, *Mexican-American Education Research Project*, 1967 (Los Angeles: California State Department of Education, 1967); "School Bias Toward Mexican-Americans," *School & Society*, Nov. 12, 1966, pp. 378, 380; and William S. Svoboda, "Negative Aspects of Education Programs for the Culturally Deprived," *School & Society*, Nov. 12, 1966, pp. 388–389.

9. Reported in Steiner, *op. cit.*, p. 212.

6

Leaning Toward Reform

What is good for the Mexican-American educationally is also good for the entire educational system. Meeting the needs of the Chicano learner will provide for an intercultural learning experience and enrich the total curriculum. The acting out of the pluralistic imperative will eventuate in a secure place in the schools for the Chicano and the reciprocal contribution of brown culture to the schools.

How is this to be done? Rivera and Cordova recommend that all school personnel and community members should seek to implement the following objectives:

1. To develop in students a sense of pride in their own cultural heritage as well as a respect for other cultures.
2. To enable students to function in another language and culture as well as in English.
3. To nurture self-reliance, innovativeness, discipline, and personal satisfaction through individualized learning activities and experiences.
4. To encourage and emphasize the beauty and strength of cultural pluralism as a model for society.[1]

If professional educators seriously pursued these objectives, the widespread failure of the schools to educate the brown learner might become a thing of the past. The schools simply must attempt to meet the needs of brown students instead of perpetually endeavoring to fit the student to the school.

There have been some stirrings in the way of moving toward an education for the Chicano that articulates honestly with his identity. Perhaps the small changes reflect the recent Mexican-American political involvement. Whatever the reason, it is worth pointing to the developing trends that could possibly evolve into authentic Chicano learning.

Congress has recognized the significance of Spanish instruction by passing Title VII of the Elementary and Secondary Education Act of 1965.[2] Title VII encourages the teaching of Spanish in the schools. Grants under the title can be used for developing bilingual education programs. In such programs, Mexican-American students study both Spanish and English. Bilingual education is at its best in schools with both Spanish- and English-speaking students; that is, in a multi-cultural context. Spanish-speaking students can learn to comprehend and speak English while English speakers can learn to understand and speak Spanish. Although this situation is optimal, a bilingual education program in a monolingual school or classroom is also pedagogically sound.

Bilingual education is not an American innovation. Bilingual curricula are extant throughout the world. Bilingual education thrives in such countries as Belgium, Canada, France, the Soviet Union, Peru, Paraguay, and Mexico. Unfortunately, American schools, although their students represent the entire spectrum of cultures, have almost completely ignored the possibilities of bilingual education. This is tragic in a nation where young people need to speak a number of dialects and languages to ensure high-quality social relations and intergroup harmony throughout the society. A viable, coherent society can only be achieved through multilingual, multicultural educational environments.

Bilingual education achieves five basic purposes for the Chicano learner and the school he attends:

1. It reduces retardation through ability to learn with the mother tongue immediately.

2. It reinforces the relations of the school and the home through a common communication bond.

3. It projects the individual into an atmosphere of personal identification, self-worth, and achievement.

4. It gives the student a base for success in the field of work.

5. It preserves and enriches the cultural and human resources of a people.[3]

A number of reading programs for Mexican-American children have been established that offer hope. An outstanding one has been ERMAS, Experiment in Reading for Mexican-American Students, a Title III Elementary and Secondary Education Act project in Corpus Christi, Texas.[4] The designers of ERMAS recognized that children learn to read more easily in their native language than they do in a different dialect or language.[5] The Chicano child's task of learning to read should not be complicated by requiring him to read in a foreign language. His first task should be restricted to the conversion of the printed word into a spoken form that he recognizes. Thus, the beginning reading program is in

Spanish although taught in the same manner as the program to be used for teaching the reading of English. In
ERMAS, while the child learns to read in Spanish, he
also learns to speak English.[6]

There is substantial evidence to indicate that bilingual
education programs can be successful. The U.S. Office of
Education reviewed the seventy-six bilingual education
projects initially funded under the Elementary and
Secondary Education Act's Title VII in 1969. Its report
demonstrated that non-English-speaking children in bilingual programs gain substantially in proficiency both in
English and in the mother tongue. Mexican-American
children in bilingual education programs learn respect
for Mexican-American culture and the Spanish language.
This leads to the Mexican-American student's more positive self-concept and eventually to better social and
personal adjustment. In the bilingual programs, the
Chicano learner advances well in school and attains to
grade-level achievement in every subject area.[7]

Culturally sensitive teacher training is critical to the
success of Spanish-English bilingual education. Teacher
training institutions must require their graduates to become fluent in both Spanish and English and competent
in the teaching of their areas of specialization in both
languages. It is patently obvious that colleges of education must train bilingual teachers if we are to have
bilingual programs.

Prospective teachers must take courses in Mexican and
Mexican-American history and culture. They should
visit the barrio and become conversant with the Chicano
life there. Teacher educators should arrange for resource
people from the Chicano community to meet with the
professional education students. The college of education

and the Chicano community must merge as much as possible. If the college is of, by, and for the Chicano community, its graduates will more effectively serve Chicano learning needs.

The Spanish language course that education students take should emphasize conversation, as taught by instructors who have enjoyed intimate, long-term experience in the barrio. The learning of the language should not be isolated from its eventual use in the classroom. Theory and practice must be fused in the study of Spanish if the teacher graduate is to command more than tourist language proficiency. As much as feasible, the prospective teacher should learn and polish his Spanish by living in the barrio and teaching in Spanish. In this way he will learn slang and nuances of meaning that he would not have learned from even the best professionals at the university.

A few colleges of education have offered innovative programs for future teachers of Chicano pupils, especially in Texas, Florida, and California. But much more, particularly in the realm of increasing the number of institutions involved, can be done.

Manuel Ramirez III, associate professor of Mexican-American studies at the University of California at Riverside, stresses that successful reform programs for the Chicano learner must include the following features:

Active Parent Involvement. Parent participation is particularly indispensable in bilingual programs, for in most Chicano communities parents have considerable knowledge of language and heritage. Parents should be remunerated to serve as language and history teachers, both at home and at school, and curriculum should be developed in such a way that parents can teach portions of it to their children at home. The Mexican-American parent will support the goals and values of the school when the school begins to recognize the worth of his culture and realize that he can make unique contributions to the educational process.

Mexican and Mexican-American Heritage Curriculum. Social studies units should include materials on Indians of Central and South America, Spanish colonization of the Southwest, heroes and historical events in Mexico, as well as the contributions of Mexican-Americans to the development of this country. These materials not only help the Chicano child develop a positive self-image but they also eliminate for Anglos the unfortunate stereotypes and misinformation that have been perpetrated by the mass media.

Culture Matching Curricula and Teaching Styles. The content of the curriculum and the teaching strategies used should be tailored to the unique learning and incentive-motivational styles of Chicano children. Moreover, these styles should conform to results of research conducted on Mexican-American children and their parents. For example, research comparing socialization practices used by Mexican-American and Anglo-American mothers of the same socio-economic class showed that Chicano mothers were more nurturing toward and protective of their children. They also encouraged them to be more dependent on and loyal to the family.[8]

The American educational establishment has evinced perceptible signs of reforming to meet the distinctive needs of brown learners. The tenets of cultural pluralism we espouse constitute the moral imperative for continued and enlarged reform. Educators, if they will but capitalize upon the rich educational resource of Chicano culture and the Spanish language, can generate a renaissance in the schools for brown learners.

NOTES

1. Feliciano Rivera and Hector L. Cordova, "Curriculum and Materials for Bilingual, Bicultural Education," *The National Elementary Principal,* Vol. L, No. 2 (November, 1970), p. 56. Copyright 1970, National Association of Elementary School Principals, NEA. All rights reserved. Reprinted by permission. For a full discussion of these scholars' ideas, see Hector L. Cordova, "The Social Psychology of the Mexican American," in Elihu Carranza, Feliciano Rivera, and H. L. Cordova, *Perspectives in Mexican American Studies* (Holt, Rinehart and Winston, Inc., 1971); and Hector L. Cordova, "Towards a Conceptual Framework for Understanding the Mexican American and Its Implication for Curriculum Development," *San Jose State College Symposium, New Directions in Mexican American Education,* May 8, 1970.

2. The original bill was introduced by two senators from a state with a large Chicano population—former Senator Ralph Yarborough and Senator John Tower, both of Texas.

3. "Toward an Advantaged Society: Bilingual Education in the '70s," *The National Elementary Principal,* Vol. L, No. 2 (November, 1970), p. 27. Copyright 1970, National Association of Elementary School Principals, NEA. All rights reserved. Reprinted by permission. For more information about bilingual programs, write Bilingual Education, Division of Plans and Supplementary Centers, Office of Education, 400 Maryland Avenue, S.W., Washington, D.C. 20202.

4. Corpus Christi Independent School District, *Experiment in Reading for Mexican American Students* (Corpus Christi Schools, June, 1967).

5. For empirical corroboration, see Nancy Modiano, *A Comparative Study of Two Approaches to the Teaching of Reading in the National Language,* Cooperative Research Project No. S-237, U.S. Department of Health, Education, and Welfare, Office of Education (New York University, 1966), and The International Institute of Teachers College, *A Survey of the Public Educational System of Puerto Rico* (Bureau of Publications, Teachers College, Columbia University, 1966).

6. Robert L. Hillerich, "ERMAS: A Beginning Reading Program for Mexican-American Children," *The National Elementary Principal,* Vol. L, No. 2 (November, 1970), pp. 80–85. Also, see Texas Education Agency, *Addresses and Reports Presented at the Conference on Development of Bilingualism in Children of Varying Linguistic and Cultural Heritages* (Austin: Texas Education Agency, February, 1967).

7. Reported in "Bilingual Education," *The National Elementary Principal,* Vol. L, No. 2 (November, 1970), p. 106.

8. Manuel Ramirez III, "Cultural Democracy: A New Philosophy for Educating the Mexican American Child," *The National Elementary Principal,* Vol. L, No. 2 (November, 1970), p. 46. Copyright 1970, National Association of Elementary School Principals, NEA. All rights reserved. Reprinted by permission.

III

BLACK DEMANDS
FOR BETTER EDUCATION

This section is hopeful. It is based on the assumption that a racially integrated society is possible, despite the American experience of violence, unkept promises, and exploitation. Several articles included present rather sorry case studies of racial conflict and discrimination. For example, the author's research on schools in New York, East St. Louis and Cairo, Illinois, and Richmond and Berkeley, California, demonstrate a number of the deep-seated social and educational problems. But cautious idealism and optimistic recommendations are not lacking. The limited success of the civil rights movement of the '60s justifies guarded hope. We can make our educational institutions accountable to black Americans if we will. By acting upon purposeful social criticism, we can create tolerant learning climates that will eventually contribute to a more pluralistic, racially harmonious society.

7

An Inquiry Into a University's "Noble Savage" Program

The study reported below * evaluates one university's educational opportunity program for blacks. The findings effectively constitute a paradigm of what is happening at most institutions of higher learning administering such programs. Illinois State University's High Potential Program is actually no worse than most. In fact, as a result of the internal dialogue that this article precipitated, the program has been much reformed so that today it is, according to independent evaluation, one of the best in the nation.

Many American universities have attempted to respond to the educational needs of blacks by establishing educational opportunity programs to assist them to secure a higher education. They recruit black students, particularly from metropolitan ghettos, and provide them financial, tutorial, and counseling assistance throughout their college careers. The goal is to compensate as much as possible for the student's deficient educational background and his lack of access to adequate funds for

* Originally appeared in *Integrated Education*, Vol. VIII, No. 4 (July–Aug., 1970), pp. 4–9. Reprinted by permission.

college so that he may successfully compete in a university and earn a degree.

What do the blacks think of such programs? The writer sought to supply at least a partial answer to this question by examining a large Midwestern university's educational opportunity program, similar to those organized by universities throughout the nation. The program in question, Illinois State University's High Potential Program, like most others, recruits talented blacks, provides them scholarships, remedially tutors, and intensively counsels them. Of 410 blacks enrolled at the university, 225 participate in the program. The writer conducted taped, in-depth interviews with a random sample of 73 of the educational opportunity students during December of 1969 and January of 1970, using an inventory schedule he had developed in order to standardize the interviews. (Twenty-seven of an initially selected one hundred refused interviews.) The results are quite revealing. The blacks do not esteem the High Potential Program.[1] They regard the program as a sort of "Noble Savage" program, a term that will, in due course, become clear.

Sixty-nine percent of the blacks resent the High Potential Program. Most dislike accepting "white money" to attend a virtually all-white institution. They are infused with the "Black Power" vision expressed in most militant form by Stokely Carmichael, H. Rap Brown, and Eldridge Cleaver. Fifty-seven percent advocate separatism as the solution to the American racial crisis. They feel trapped in a black ghetto within the university; they would prefer their own educational institution which they could control. They believe the "pseudo-liberal cry for integration," to quote one respondent's phrase, is based on the assumption that "blacks are too stupid to learn without a white kid being around." After all, they say, who wants to attend school with a lot of sick racists? Better to be with blacks, even if the buildings are dilapidated and the staff underpaid, than be treated like a "plantation nigger." As one black put it: "Man, I want to be with my own people. I'm here because I can't afford to pay to go to school and mostly because it makes whites feel better."

Forty-seven percent of the blacks fear they will begin to think white. The recent movement toward an appreciation of black culture and beauty has greatly impressed them. They believe they have a cultural past, developed painfully in a repressive and alien culture, that is worth preserving. They do not want to be "brainwashed" by a white institution. They regard the High Potential Program as nothing more than a way of trapping them in a white university, a carrot dangled on a big stick by "Uncle Toms" and "fake liberals."

Assumed Inferiority

What do blacks resent specifically about the educational opportunity program? Their most poignant criticism is that the High Potential Program operates on the assumption that Negroes are inferior—the supposition that "the culturally disadvantaged require a special program to compensate for their deficiencies." They are ambivalent at best about receiving help to succeed in an educational system that even hints at their inferiority. One dashiki-garbed student, fingering a carved black fist dangling about his neck, complains: "It's about time they gave us scholarships just like they do for whites.

They don't have to set up a ghetto on campus for us, except that it points out to us that we're getting a hand-out." The High Potential students feel conspicuous and experience considerable stigma. One problem is vocal groups of white students who express or imply their belief that every black on campus benefits from the program, which is not the case. Black tends to be equated with "High Potential student," unfortunately code for "black student on welfare."

The blacks surveyed also resent virtually exclusive use of white tutors for black students. The seriousness of this issue is indicated by the fact that 91 percent of the blacks want black tutors and claim that many of the present corps of tutors cannot relate to the needs of blacks. A sophomore coed claims: "My tutor can't teach me much because he thinks I am a black who is here to become white. His attitude prevents learning." Eighty-six percent of the blacks express the desire to control the hiring of their own tutors.

Many blacks are particularly sensitive about the university's special criteria for admitting talented blacks who do not satisfy regular admission standards. Forty-one percent maintain that the criteria are excessively subjective, almost political: straight, conservative types are over-selected because the racist administration fears Black Panther types invading the student union or participating in conspicuous interracial dating. Thirty-five percent of the respondents believe that the internal logic of the university necessitates brandishing the liberal rhetoric of "equality and justice forever" while actually doing as little as possible to promote change. Over three quarters of the sample charge the educational opportunity program with hypocrisy. They feel the special admission policy is part of the university's duplicity. The data clearly demonstrate, however, that if special admissions are intended to bring only compatible and contented blacks to the university, the plan has failed miserably. Most of the High Potential students are openly critical.

FEEL BOUGHT

Fifty-seven percent of the educational opportunity students interviewed express varying degrees of guilt about having accepted financial and tutorial help. There seems to be a basic conflict between their acceptance of white assistance and the reality of their ambivalence or dislike for white institutions. Attendance at Illinois State University is a financial necessity—not a matter of choice with those interviewed. Almost 70 percent of the blacks would rather attend such all-black schools as Fisk or Howard. Consequently, many students feel they have bartered their dignity for security and advancement. It is perhaps this guilt or malaise, this sense of having "sold out," that is a major cause of the black disaffection from the High Potential Program.

Despite the Negro students' negativism toward white institutions, the educational opportunity students are academically as successful as other students in terms of grade point average and the completion of the standard four-year program. The black High Potential students may be irritated with the university, but they do not allow their emotions to depress their academic performance. And 88 percent of the respondents emphasize that the university is their only realistic hope for upward social mobility. Seventy-four percent even concede that the

High Potential Program is producing some positive results. Although they are all at least nominal advocates of "Black Power," the blacks are willing to compromise themselves, albeit grudgingly, in order to secure the education they regard as absolutely essential for success. A good number (29 percent) wish to return to their communities after graduation to work for the amelioration of their brothers' condition and are particularly able to justify what many regard as complicity in an educational opportunity program. They argue that they are "using" the program in the cause of black self-improvement.

Although an overwhelming majority of black scholarship students dislike or are ambivalent about both the High Potential Program and the university itself, some blacks are less negative than others. The juniors and seniors are less negative about the program and the college experience than sophomores and freshmen. This suggests that a socialization process may be operative: the blacks, many recruited directly from Chicago and East St. Louis ghettos and unaccustomed to an integrated educational experience, may increasingly feel comfortable in what is initially a very alien environment. One freshman says, "When I got here this fall, man, I was so uptight I wanted to quit school and go home." A senior woman reflects on four years: "When I came here, there were just a few blacks—today, over four hundred. I like it better here with more blacks, but I also feel different about whites. Some are my friends, but not my best friends." Nevertheless, despite attitude changes, the prevailing black viewpoint is more typical of an exploited colonial people than of an upwardly mobile group.

WOMEN MOST AGGRIEVED

Black women are more resentful of the High Potential Program than black men. This attitude may be integral to the black woman's more general sense of alienation from the university social milieu.[2] The women feel constricted in their social life. They are as interested in marriage as any woman, but they perceive the supply of eligible black men as being exceedingly small. They would much prefer to be at Howard University, or some other predominantly black institution, where there is an advantageous sex ratio, and where virtually every man is training for a profession.

Two thirds of the black students also feel that the High Potential Program is a device for treating them differently and indicating tacitly that they would be wise to refrain from excessive interracial contact, especially dating and sex. This situation is flushed with dualism: the blacks are alienated to such an extent that they would rather be elsewhere but they also feel excluded. They want the freedom and economic power to determine their own style of education.

Seventy-one percent of the sample plan careers in teaching, social welfare, government, and librarianship. They explain that discrimination against Negroes is less in these fields than others, most emphatically business. They want to complete a major that leads to remunerative employment. The median income of the students' parents is $5,300. Two percent of the families rank above the $10,000 level and 14 percent below $3,000. Seventy-seven percent of the students come from either East St. Louis or the Chicago area. Fifteen percent of the students report that the mother is the only parent in the household. Only one student reports that the father is the only parent in the home. Seventeen percent of the students' families receive some sort of welfare subsidy such as Aid to Dependent Children. The High Potential students have, by every indicator, suffered privation and poverty. Their modest career plans are typical for a generation emerging from the poverty and brutality of the ghetto.

PROTEST MADE POSSIBLE

One of the unintended results of the educational opportunity program has been the raising of the black voice of protest on campus. The High Potential Program has made black protest a physical possibility by doubling the number of blacks on campus. Their protest seems often, however, to be directed as much to releasing the anger blacks have historically turned inward and emancipating the cramped inner self than achieving positive reform, or even revolution, for that matter. They have protested in such ways as occupying the Illinois State University library and storming the flagpole to lower the flag to half-mast in honor of slain Illinois Black Panther leader Fred Hampton. Such tactics are dramatic, and may win local campus battles, but their long-term impact is counter-productive. Contemporary black student protest is, like college protest generally, very much like "guerrilla theater": it shocks Everyman's sensibilities; it deeply involves the ego, eliciting a histrionic catharsis; and, it often constitutes a do-it-yourself psychotherapy.

The blacks at Illinois State have transcended protest to

some extent by organizing a Black Student Association (BSA) as an organ for collectively wielding an independent political force. The BSA's activities have upset some white students, who are primarily from rural backgrounds and little experienced in interracial contact. A group of infuriated whites, disgusted with the black arguments that the selection of the homecoming queen is racially biased and the president of the university is a bigot, established a counter-organization, the Blond Student Association (also BSA).

Fifty-two percent of the educational opportunity students resent the fact that they always seem to be officially identified as "Negro students" rather than merely "students." Many pointed to this as prima-facie evidence of the structural racism of the university. Thirty-one percent even think that the High Potential Program is integral to the very anatomy of white racism. The program buttresses what they regard as a covert "separate but equal" university policy; that is, the university provides compensatory education and financial assistance, but continues to operate on the assumption of Negro intellectual inferiority and helplessness. The red-neck image of the "watermelon-eating darky" has been supplanted by the ideology (almost a cult) of the "culturally deprived" and "socially disadvantaged" in the minds of white educators. The new rationalizations are based historically upon Jean Jacques Rousseau's celebration of the "noble savage," the simple, undefiled primitive who had a certain dignity and grandeur despite his technological backwardness and lack of high culture. Viewed from this perspective, the educational opportunity program becomes a "Noble Savage" program, a type of modern colonial outpost where the most noble (meaning most like white) blacks can be fed and instructed in the white man's ways.

MOST DISAPPROVING BLACKS

The blacks who most disapprove of the High Potential Program share certain characteristics. They are the most academically successful and think of themselves as independent of white benevolence. Participation in the educational opportunity program does not constitute an admission that they cannot make it through college without help. The blacks believe they could succeed in other ways, but there would be more obstacles to overcome. The most indignant blacks major in the social sciences and humanities. They attended primarily segregated inner-city high schools. The few physical education, math, and science majors seem to be a uniquely contented group. They also had a predominantly segregated high school experience. The several blacks (14 percent) who had participated in civil rights activities all express an aversion to the High Potential Program. One explains: "This program is like the OEO's war on poverty. Most of the money goes to the bureaucrats for administration or is used for the wrong things."

A small percentage of the students interviewed espouse extreme versions of the general criticism of the educational opportunity program. Most whites would regard their opinions as unfounded, albeit noteworthy. Four blacks accuse the university of supporting a program, actually intended, despite the humanistic rhetoric, to siphon potential leadership from the Black Power Movement and to "rape the black community" (one respondent's words), plundering its most valuable human resource. Almost one quarter of the sample believe that the educational opportunity program is designed basically to protect the vulnerable university from attack.

An educational opportunity program is today a *sine qua non* for meeting the black challenge to the relevance and legitimacy of the university. (A conservative faculty member rationalized the program, saying, "We must have the High Potential Program and black studies courses, at least until this Black Power thing blows over.") A final argument expressed by six of the informants emphasizes that the High Potential Program is a device for quarantining young blacks who might seek to promote significant social change.

The term "Noble Savage" program hints at the paternalism and hypocrisy that blacks attribute to Illinois State University's educational opportunity program. The intent of the expression is not basically polemical but heuristic: it may be able to jolt some rigid, authoritarian personalities and stimulate humanistic policy. We must realize that the minority students who benefit from our programs designed to integrate them into the university's world of opportunities and upward mobility do not necessarily entertain the same image of the programs as we do. We must seek to promote thoughtful dialogue and cooperative effort between black students and white faculty, administrators, and students so that mutually agreeable adjustments in the purpose and governance of the opportunity programs can be made. The university community has subtly defamed blacks by failing to consult them regarding the structure and operation of what is really *their* program. This limited study demonstrates that the blacks think there is much wrong with the present method of administering educational opportunity to them. If the findings are valid elsewhere, a comprehensive reorganization of programs is patently in order.

NOTES

1. This study's research findings are generally consistent with previous findings that black students are not favorably inclined toward a number of aspects of their university experience. The studies in which these findings appear include Aaron M. Bindman's "Participation of Negro Students in an Integrated University," unpublished Ph.D. dissertation in sociology, University of Illinois, Urbana, 1965, and Evelyn R. Rosenthal's "The Differential Perceptions of Negro and White Undergraduates at an Integrated Institution," unpublished M.A. thesis in sociology, University of Illinois, Urbana, 1968. Nathan Hare maintains that middle-class blacks are more interested in parallel institutions modeled upon white ones than integrated solutions to racial problems. (*The Black Anglo-Saxons;* Marzani & Munsell, Inc., Publishers, 1965.)

Clark and Plotkin (1963) report many findings consistent with the present data, but two of their findings are notable for their conflict with this and other studies. They explain that "the decision to enter an interracial college rather than a segregated one probably reflects a tendency or conscious desire to break through the existing racial barriers." (Kenneth B. Clark and Lawrence Plotkin, *The Negro Student at Integrated Colleges,* p. 20; National Scholarship Service and Fund for Negro Students, 1963.) They also note the blacks' "generally positive attitude towards college experiences . . . confirmed by the practically unanimous rejection of the statement expressing regret at having attended an interracial college" (*ibid.,* p. 28). It is perhaps possible that there has been a significant shift in young blacks' attitudes during the seven years.

2. Bindman found black women to be more dissatisfied with their social life than black men.

8

The Chimera of Open Admissions

The City University of New York initiated in the fall of 1970 an "open admissions" program. Through this program, every graduating senior in the New York City high schools may have, if he wishes, a place in the university. The program allows for 19 percent of graduating high school seniors entering the senior colleges, 26 percent studying in the community colleges, and another 20 percent or more pursuing the higher learning in "educational skills centers," a genre of training that culminates in low-paying hospital, clerical, and teaching-aid positions.[1] The New York City Board of Higher Education informed the colleges that they were to, under the open admissions plan, provide remedial and supportive services for those not satisfying the conventional entrance requirements so that open admissions would not become "the illusion of an open door to higher education which in reality is only a revolving door, admitting everyone but leading to a high proportion of student failure after one semester." The board also charged the City University system with the responsibility for the "ethnic integration of the university" so that there would be no *de facto*-segregated institutions, especially heavily disproportionate minority enrollment in the community colleges, within the City University system. And finally, perhaps the board's most difficult challenge, the system was given the responsibility to "maintain and enhance the standards of academic excellence of the colleges of the University." [2] Although there are no hard data yet available to assess the degree to which these objectives have been realized, there are some major indicators that enable preliminary examination, analysis, and speculation.

THE TRACKING SCENARIO

Because of educational tracking, the whole of American society has become, contrary to the popular mythology, increasingly stratified. With unprecedented regularity, Americans enter their fathers' occupations or ones with comparable prestige and income. Family income is the basic determinant of educational achievement. Thus, a cycling effect is operative: the father finances the son's education and the son, in turn, attains the status or occupational level of his father. This situation constitutes a patrimony of education and income because seldom does the education per se prepare the learner for his job. The learner is hired rather for the prestige of his degree rather than its relevance to the job. Patricia Sexton summarizes the societal-educational tracking aptly: "There is, in fact, an absence of evidence that the most able in performance of jobs or other real-life tasks are selected or produced by the standards set and training offered by higher education. Employers often hire from among the degree elite because of the prestige rather than the superior training or job performance skill attached to a college degree." [3] If employers do really seek prestige rather than skill and competence, one wonders if the open admissions policy, if effective, might render the employers' preference for degree holders less tenable. A recent Carnegie Commission of Higher Education study discovered that children from families whose incomes exceed the national median are three times more likely to enter college than children below the median. [4] If this class stratification in education were terminated or seriously impeded, employers might rely more heavily on their own criteria. One of these is, of course, skin color.

Vociferous minority groups have become highly sensitized to the disparity between the rhetoric of social mobility and pernicious systems of tracking. [5] They have demanded both the abolition of tracking and open admissions to colleges. They stress that tracking becomes increasingly invidious as the occupational structure becomes more complex: a lower-level track now often leads to unemployment rather than low-status work. The critics point out that jobs requiring no secondary education have decreased 25 percent in the past ten years. In contrast, white-collar workers, who composed 15 percent of the work force in 1900 and 28.5 percent in 1940, [6] will constitute over half by 1975. [7] Thus, the lower tracks are not only stigmatized, they are increasingly unproductive. The imperative for the abolition of tracking is, therefore, managerial; business requires highly trained personnel who can fill slots in a complex economy. The blacks, Puerto Ricans, and Chicanos have absorbed the lion's share of tracking punishment to date and they are now finding the treatment even more brutal. They, the great unwashed, want out and up.

Nonwhites, most of them poor, constituted 40 percent of New York City's high school student population in 1967. They made up 60 percent of the "vocational" high school student bodies and 36 percent of the students in the academic high school populations. In Brooklyn Tech and the Bronx High School of Science, elite institutions that demand high qualifying scores for admissions, nonwhites total only 12 percent and 7 percent of the students respectively. Tracking is evident in these statistics, but the most significant impact is discernible in the data for students in the academic high schools. The vast majority of blacks and Puerto Ricans fill lower tracks that culminate in "general" rather than "academic" diplomas. A mere 18 percent of the academic high school graduates were black or Puerto Rican. It is certainly not extravagantly charitable and libertarian to abolish entrance requirements when only 18 percent of the high school graduates are black or Puerto Rican. Of the 18 percent who graduated, only one fifth entered college, compared with a 63 percent figure for whites who graduated. Therefore, only 7 percent of the 1967 graduates of New York's academic high schools who entered college were black or Puerto Rican. The data [8] document that tracking in New York has been especially pernicious on the high school level, almost totally nullifying any possible benefits of an open admissions policy.

THE MILITARY OPTION

As the open admissions students begin to graduate in 1974, the ratio of unemployed and underemployed blacks to appropriate job opportunities will increase. As this ratio increases, a related phenomenon will occur with greater frequency; that is, educated blacks will discover that their major viable occupational alternative is military service. Undoubtedly, many, seeking a sanctioned outlet for their aspirations, will take advantage of the military option. They will become professional Black Hessians, but they will be chronically dissatisfied, given their awareness of the constraints of their subordinate social position, in a role that is not comparable to that of whites with the same education. Their consciousness of American society's structural discrimination will not abate. In fact, there is evidence that the sense of powerlessness and anger will be reinforced in the Armed Forces. A study of the attitudes of black GI's and officers in Vietnam detected a flood tide of bitterness.[9] For example, only 37.8 percent of the black enlisted men concurred that weapons have *no* place in the struggle for their rights in the United States. Fifty percent indicated they would use weapons, while 13 percent responded that they would organize guerrilla military units. The vast majority of black soldiers feel that America will experience an increasingly violent racial crisis during the '70s. Most respondents were willing to participate in rioting as a last-ditch measure to focus public scrutiny on their grievances.[10] A society that cannot or will not use its black college graduates, at all or to capacity, buttresses this pattern of alienation and predisposition to direct action and violence. Open admissions is, in this perspective, irrelevant to the ultimate solution of the racial crisis. The problem is not really subject to a solely educational cure. In an occupationally "upgrading" society, one demanding more education for the same job, open admissions will only serve to render the minority graduate's lack of a productive role in the social order

an extremely embittering condition. In short, the economic structure of racism will effectively negate the
educational reform of open admissions.

CAMPUS PROTEST FOR OPEN CAMPUSES

Campus radicals, the youthful exponents of affluent
America's guilt-ridden "conscience constituency," [11] supported, in some cases promoted, minority demands for
an opening up, a leavening, of the monolithic, single-
standard system. Bitter crises at San Francisco State, the
University of Illinois, and the City College of New York,
among others, were precipitated by the issue of minority
representation in the student body. Underground research groups documented the machinations of the
tracking system, demonstrating in each case how the
minorities and poor are "channeled" (the reports often
parodied Selective Service jargon) into the terminal
community or junior colleges while the white middle
class, from kindergarten on, is counseled, cajoled, and
cosseted into the prestige-enhancing and job-getting
universities. The reality set impolitely down beside the
rhetoric threw numerous campuses across the nation into
violent convulsions over the social question of "Who is to
be educated?"

The protest movement on the New York City senior
college campuses made an open admissions policy a
strategic necessity. Reactionaries mobilized to abort the
policy. Politicians, trustees, wealthy influentials, and
other sources of bigotry lobbied the colleges to "maintain
standards," not to "capitulate to the demands of demon-
strators." [12] And by "standards" these advocates meant
the class and economic privilege built into those "stan-

dards." The legislators in Albany could neither comprehend nor sense the threat of total anarchy and social
holocaust on location that impelled even ritualistic, conservative faculty members and administrators to accede
reluctantly to open admissions. But administrators and
faculty members on the scene knew, although many
were apprehensive, that some sort of open admissions
program was timely if the senior colleges were to survive. They managed to win the day. Thus, in very large
measure, the open admissions policy is predicated upon
enlightened self-interest and political expediency: there
existed a great need to import a modicum of tranquillity
onto the campus so that teaching could continue, the
paychecks would keep coming, and the bulk of privileges
might be maintained. Open admissions was simply the
only viable alternative to the collapse of the colleges
under the cyclonic impact of the radical subcultures.

THE IMPACT OF OPEN ADMISSIONS

Although the representatives of privilege and special
interest attacked open admissions as a betrayal of academic standards,[13] the standards have not been abandoned, only amended. The traditional standard for the
New York senior colleges remains; but a new, alternative
criterion, a student's rank in his high school class, has
been added. Thus, a student from the incredibly inferior
ghetto schools can enter one of the senior colleges by
placing in approximately the top half of his class. Open
admissions is, therefore, not as open-ended as the rather
pejorative and hopeful term implies. A more precise, less
intimidating term would be something on the order of
"individual admissions." What has effectively happened

is that the educational valves, those institutional devices that allocate students to hieratic statuses,[14] have been moved upstairs, where they serve nominally to expiate the intense guilt of a sadomasochistically racist society by benefiting a few individuals from the groups that now so belligerently frighten us.

The impact of open admissions cannot be fully and accurately ascertained yet. The program only began in September, 1970, and no longitudinal data now exist. It is certain, however, that students, unqualified by the old criteria, are securing admission. Thirty-seven percent of the incoming freshmen at City College have high school averages below the old standard of 80 percent.[15] The college has necessarily adapted its program to the new "clientele" (bureaucratese for "students"). A number of programs have been established for students requiring "remediation." Students in need of special help are assigned to the Department of Special Programs. Learners are tested and those who score below a certain point enroll in noncredit courses in their deficient areas. For example, the Department of Special Programs offers a basic skills course in reading that a staff of fourteen teaches.[16] Such remediation efforts have been essential to open admissions. The professed aim is simultaneously to remediate and educate at the collegiate level "without sacrificing standards." This is patently a liberal chimera, fantasied in the oven of political pressure and the vacuum of ivory towerism. Open admissions has introduced (and legitimately so) a new definition of standards.[17] To speak as if the old academic standards were firmly bolted to the parapets only encourages an incipient psychosis.

Open admissions contributes in limited measure to the

remedy of flagrant injustice. The inequity that open admissions partially corrects is the disproportionate spending of public education money on the children of the suburban affluent at the expense of the poor, especially at the college level. Patricia Sexton, New York University educational sociologist, has analyzed the situation: "In general the more money a student's parents make, the more money will be spent on his education, despite some efforts at public 'compensatory' expenditures for the disadvantaged." [18] For example, prior to open admissions, New York City's tuition-free colleges with "high standards . . . have . . . subsidized many middle-income students and virtually excluded most impoverished ethnic groups." "Low college tuition," according to Sexton, "offers few opportunities to lower-income students if entrance standards are too high to hurdle." Open admissions has granted a segment of the educationally unqualified poor (who are generally unqualified because they are poor) access to the most expensive levels of public education in New York City, the senior colleges. The benefit has been somewhat counteracted by the assessment of higher fees in the graduate programs, but there will probably be a net, positive effect. However, this small effect will be more than fully negated by larger societal processes.

THE "UPGRADING" DILEMMA

The open admissions policy, professedly humanistic (there is a grain of altruism in the policy), and the societal process of "job upgrading" (the inflation of educational requirements for the same job), now occurring at an accelerating rate, are on collision courses. If an impoverished, open admissions student works assiduously to get an education, but still occupies a socioeconomic position that is inferior to that of whites with equivalent education, a status that may not, in fact, be significantly different from his social origin, he is in as bad shape, especially psychologically, as if he had never attended college. There is excellent evidence to sustain the hypothesis that this will be the case under the open admissions plan. For example, 35 percent of the nonwhites over eighteen years of age had finished four years of high school in 1965 and 7 percent had finished college, but only 17 percent were in professional, technical, managerial, clerical, and sales positions, a percentage much less than that of whites with similar educational backgrounds.[19] The horrid reality is that tracking is absolutely essential to the preservation of the social and occupational structure as it now exists. Hence, equality of educational opportunity cannot mean equality of socioeconomic opportunity. A transformation of the present welfare state would be required for the latter type of opportunity. Once this becomes apparent, dissident students will blow the roof off the New York senior colleges. The image that fits this Sisyphean dilemma, which the radicals will soon seize upon, is the squirrel in a circular cage: the faster the squirrel runs, the less he moves. Thus, although open admissions may seem to indulge the socioeconomically depressed's aspirations for upward mobility, it may in fact be accomplishing little more than keeping volatile campuses from blowing up. Unfortunately, the lid cannot remain on too long once the structural contradiction of an open admissions policy set in the context of an upgrading occupational structure becomes fully operative and visible.

THE REAL FUNCTION OF OPEN ADMISSIONS

The implementation of open admissions in New York City, a hurried response to the threat of racial and ethnic crisis (1975 was the original target date), seems radical and visionary, but it is effectively only the introduction of the traditional open admissions policy of the landgrant colleges into an urban setting. A significant number of urban blacks will, for the first time, enjoy an opportunity to succeed at a level that theoretically determines largely how the good things of life are distributed. The reactionaries' image of a nineteenth-century British colonial outpost deluged by spearthrowing natives is certainly not applicable to the open admissions situation, not even at the outer limits of racial paranoia. As indicated, the open admissions program allows for only 19 percent of graduating high school seniors entering the senior colleges, 26 percent entering community colleges, and another 20 percent or more being funneled into "educational skills centers." These figures indicate a cautious resort to the open admissions option. And, to be sure, open admissions is all the more modest when one considers that only 7 percent of the graduates of the academic high schools are nonwhite. Open admissions does, in fact, perpetuate an attenuated version of tracking. A disproportionate number of students from socioeconomically depressed backgrounds will finalize their occupational fate in what Kingsley Widmer calls, in the California context, "those fancied-up super high schools, the local two-year 'community colleges.'" [20] That outcome will be a logical outgrowth of the 26 percent and 20 percent entering community colleges and "educational skills centers" respectively. The ineluctable inference is that, although open admissions diminishes tracking, it also preserves it.

The racial and ethnic participatory pluralism that to-day intimidates the WASP has compelled the open admissions accommodation. It is preferable to either confrontation or genuine minority involvement in decision-making. The WASP Establishment has granted concessions, but the crucial consideration is that they have retained control (as in the modern factories, where the management would rather paint the pipes gorgeous orange and grant handsome wage increases than contend with a belligerent union). Black and Puerto Rican welfare recipients drain the system, the managerial argument goes on; so, if we can get a token number of them both off our backs and off the welfare rolls, we shall have cunningly commandeered the incipient pluralism they have so agonizingly mobilized and also saved a few dollars. (Few dare speculate that welfare blacks and Puerto Ricans may indeed be integral to the social system.) Open admissions is, in short, when one cuts through all the liberal rhetoric and crocodile tears, an instrument of co-optation directed toward groups that threaten the social order and the injustice and privilege it represents.

Timothy S. Healy, vice-chancellor of academic affairs at the City University, has justified the open admissions plan as an "interrupter of poverty." [21] Subjected to critical inquiry, this argument is revealed basically as a liberal facade for a program designed to anesthetize angry subcultures that could not at one time and now will not fade away into the vaunted "melting pot." Open admissions seeks to incorporate the blacks and other minorities into the same antiquated and decrepit institutions that mollified, in part satisfied, the intense aspirations of the city's earlier in-migrants. It deflects the incisive criticism that insists on a humanized society of pluralism and equality, where none suffer abuse and denial and everyone authenticates himself in terms of his genuine identity. It is, in effect, a reform offered to the militants so they can become socially mobile if they work sufficiently hard. This is the sense in which it is an "interrupter of poverty." The work ethic and the inequality, the meritocracy and the melting pot are thereby defended in one super-liberal reform. But nothing substantial changes.

Vice-Chancellor Healy presented the rationale for open admissions in a *Saturday Review* article:

> The poverty line may not rise in absolute dollars, but without a significant increase in our pools of educated men and women it will surely swell in absolute numbers. When I was a youngster, you needed a college degree to run an elevator in Radio City (although ironically you didn't need one to work in the Public Library), and the day may come when we will have to address telephone operators as "Madam Doctor." But unless all the city's people can keep pace with this process, we are building the city's death into the future. We are also, perhaps more important, tolerating a total of human anguish and frustration that will mark us as history's most unfeeling people.[22]

On the contrary. To invite poor, nonwhite students, caught up in the international revolution of rising expectations,[23] onto the treadmill of meritocratic education is to be immeasurably "unfeeling." It is to promote the worst possible consequences. To raise an oppressed people's aspirations through an educational system that presently generates an intellectual proletariat of unemployed degree holders is to threaten the society's viability more than if the open admissions reform had never been attempted. We cannot in good conscience tell poor, black, high school graduates reading at an average seventh- to eighth-grade level, that they need Ph.D.'s for decent jobs. In an era when numerous Ph.D.'s are unemployed or underemployed and the society is straining under the financial burden of education, how credible and worthwhile will a frustrated young black find the vice-chancellor's analysis?

The ultimate in humanistic educational policy would be to pronounce candidly that we shall no longer subject learners to inordinate schooling. Much of it serves, in any case, no other purpose than to legitimize the ideologies of progress and work. Unfortunately, Vice-Chancellor Healy's commentary discloses that officially there is really nothing structurally innovative in open admissions; the conventional lockstep hierarchy into oblivion remains stably in place on the launching pad.

The Structural Flaw of Open Admissions

It is virtually a foregone conclusion that open admissions will have no significant impact on the cycle of poverty in New York. It would be incongruous if it did. For example, public expenditures on education in the '60s increased at a rate faster than that of the gross national product, but the most impoverished Americans were never touched by the spending.[24] The competitive necessity of getting more education for the same job has absorbed any potential benefit to the poor of increased expenditures. The stark reality is that, even if the schools were so structured as to favor minorities, the insecure and exploitative society would enervate the minorities' educational advancement. Riesman and Jencks write:

> So long as the distribution of power and prestige remain radically unequal, so long as some children are raised by adults at the top, the children will more often than not, turn out unequal. . . . We suspect that these differences account for more of the class variation in college changes than all other differences combined.[25]

What is desperately needed is a society that is not premised upon extreme polarities of wealth and power, but one that operates on the basis of equality rather than mobility.

Nowhere in the open admissions policy has the assumption that each increment of education causes an increment of prestige, income, and job advancement been questioned. This is the pivotal fallacy.[26] Additional years of formal education have no real, intrinsic correlation with a better job and salary. (Any unemployed Ph.D. can tell you that much.) The link has been a contrived one, such as the link between marijuana use and the supposed natural transition to harder stuff, for example, heroin. As in the putative drug cycle, the link in education is a type of "pusher." He is called an "educator." The educational pusher is a professional in whose interest it is to argue that "to get a good job, stay in school." Certainly. If the students and their parents do not believe this myth, it would be impossible to elicit the willing compliance and support of the population for building educational empires. The sociological truth is that education and income are mediated by the variable of social class; a direct relationship is illusory. Thus, the believing minority student's endeavor to get ahead by obtaining a college degree is particularly abortive.

The educational professional claims, in behalf of the Educational Establishment, that those who do not meet conventional standards must be molded and educated as everyone else. There is no mention of alternatives,[27] only a reading of the litany of economic justifications for higher education. The fact is that everyone has been taken in by the professional hoax that long years of education are requisite to success. This unidimensional mentality fails to explain the many great men and women who find schooling stultifying, especially the most creative ones, such as Paul Goodman and Eric Hoffer. Open admissions, to the extent that it is open, is a passport to the practice of mythology and ritual. To date, virtually everyone has accepted the validity of the rituals (curriculum) and the authority of the priests (professors). Open admissions is an indicator that the Educational Establishment hopes it can narcotize the restive minorities, even at this late hour, in order to perpetuate the myths. But the minorities have been much too brutalized and embittered by a culturally assassinating educational system of tracking and "cooling out" (the discouragement of high aspirations by low-status students) [28] to swallow the tantalizing hypnotic.

EDUCATIONAL ALTERNATIVES

Open admissions initially damped the awareness of many suspicious blacks, but a significant number have resumed their demands for education they themselves devise and control, learning experiences that flow from their own life concerns rather than the prerogatives and interests of a burgeoning professoriat, aspiring for tenure and pasture at $30,000 a year. They claim that only when the archaic professoriat has been toppled, like the medieval churchmen, will they enjoy educational reformation and authentic dialogue. Each black is entitled, as a fundamental human right, to an education that allows him the freedom and the resources to define himself existentially. In a climate of learner freedom, the blacks would no longer be particularly anxious to emulate the white's educational style but would rely on their own inner and cultural resources to fashion self-fulfilling, culturally expressive educational experiences.[29] Thus, the reform that should precede open admissions, one that would make that term meaningful, is open education, an educational milieu of alternatives, wherein each learner may pursue questions that help him to grapple with the problematic nature of his own human condition. The adoption of this pedagogical parameter would preclude building an education upon the managerial ethic; that is, the more one learns, the more one earns. That ethic leads to monolithic certification and a single-standard concept of expertise. Each individual would be responsible, in a milieu of existentially distinguishable alternatives, for defining himself and his education. He would be accountable only to himself. The advocates of the encrusted old standards cannot maintain their debilitating hegemony over the increasingly conscious minorities in an educational world of choices.

Potentially, the most existentially authentic educational choice for blacks and the other minorities is the independent college.[30] Only in an autonomous institution of higher education can blacks avoid the negative effects of the meritocracy upon self-reliant cultural expressiveness. In order for the independent college to become a reality, the much proposed system of tuition vouchers (variously known as educational chits or credits, and the edu-credit card) must be applied at the collegiate level. Each learner should receive an equal financial resource from the Government for his higher education. He may educate himself as he sees fit with the money, save a few basic reading and mathematical skills that would be required. In this milieu of choice, many blacks could and would pay tuition at independent colleges that eschew the concept of learning for earning in favor of a serious examination of self and society and the development of action programs that articulate honestly with these considerations. Linking black thinking with black action, black culture with black expressiveness, is the only way to open up the monolithic society the apologists portray as a melting pot. Indeed, only when black thought and culture translate into significant educational and political self-sufficiency will the meritocracy open its doors fully to black college graduates. Open admissions presupposes white domination of the curriculum and the perpetuation of the prejudicial social structure. Black, autonomous colleges, open to all and publicly funded with tuition vouchers, would constitute a major step toward both equality of educational opportunity and equality of job opportunity.

The Bitter Fruits of Reform

My rather firm inference is that the open admissions program simply accomplishes a strengthening of the monopoly of education over success. The school still functions as an instrument and guarantor of the state; it is the *sine qua non* for the insecure, achieving society. Education, piled higher and deeper, is not the answer to the problems of an urbanized nation. Formal curricula acted out within four walls, or even experiments flowing from behind the walls, cannot eliminate or significantly alleviate ethnic and racial tensions. In fact, more schooling will intensify the conflict because minority learners must achieve considerably in order to maintain the same relative position (as, in degree, everybody now must).[31] The frustration and anger generated by unrealized aspirations will become explosive; the ultimate fruits of open admissions will be bitter and violent. The social system of structural racism and inequality will be deprived of its mask when a large percentage of fully qualified black college graduates cannot escape ghettoesque unemployment and despair. Having succeeded in full measure and yet still subject to the unfeeling paranoia of institutionalized racism, these educated blacks will be revolutionized. They will become the leaders for guerrilla movements, styled after the revolutionary thoughts and programs of Fidel Castro, Ché Guevara, and Frantz Fanon, and emanating from the inner city. The unwanted by-product of open admissions, the ego- and culturally-liberating discovery that there is no future for the black beyond token participation, will contribute very probably to a cult of violence and revolution. If the ghetto becomes an armed camp, the American racial crisis will have finally dissolved the fragile bindings of the social contract. The Educational Establishment, incapable of or uninterested in imagining beyond encapsulated, chimerical reforms like open admissions, will be guilty of unpardonable complicity.

NOTES

1. New York City Board of Higher Education, "The Open Admissions Program," mimeographed (New York: Board of Higher Education, 1970), pp. 42–47.

2. Timothy S. Healy, "The Challenge of Open Admissions: Will Everyman Destroy the University?" *Saturday Review,* Dec. 20, 1969, p. 54.

3. Patricia Cayo Sexton, *The American School* (Prentice-Hall, Inc., 1967), p. 51.

4. "Higher Education for Negroes Seen Most Urgent U.S. Issue," *Chronicle of Higher Education,* Dec. 9, 1968, p. 2.

5. Paulo Freire terms this sensitivity "conscientization," the process of becoming aware of the limiting, coercive elements in one's social condition. Freire concludes that "the fundamental role of those committed to cultural action for conscientization is not properly speaking to fabricate the liberating idea, but to invite the people to grasp with their minds the truth of their reality." See *Harvard Educational Review,* August, 1970, p. 473.

6. John Vaizey and Michael Debeauvais, "Economic Aspects of Educational Development," in A. H. Halsey, J. Floud, and C. H. Anderson (eds.), *Education, Economy, and Society* (The Free Press of Glencoe, Inc., 1961), pp. 38–39.

7. D. H. Wrong, "Portrait of a Decade," *The New York Times Magazine,* Aug. 2, 1970, p. 23.

8. The New York data were obtained by Columbia University SDS, April, 1968, from the records of the New York City Board of Education, through the office of the Rev. Milton Galamison, then a board member.

9. Wallace Terry, II, "Black GI's—Bringing the War Home," *San Francisco Chronicle,* June 30, 1970, p. 13.

10. Wallace Terry, II, spent more than two years in Viet-

nam as a correspondent for *Time* magazine. He administered a 109-item inventory schedule on racial attitudes to 833 black and white servicemen as part of a private survey. His conclusions are based on 2500 scientifically comprised tables derived from the servicemen's replies by the Harvard Computer Center.

11. Michael Harrington coined the term "conscience constituency" to refer to the recent development of a group of citizens who are politically involved, in part at least, in response to ethical considerations rather than purely self-interest. See Michael Harrington, *Toward a Democratic Left: A Radical Program for a New Majority* (Penguin Books, Inc., 1969), p. 270.

12. Leonard Buder, "On Open Admissions," *The New York Times*, July 11, 1969, p. 38.

13. M. A. Farber, "Albany Leaders Cool to City U. Bid For Open-Door Aid," *The New York Times*, July 11, 1969, p. 1.

14. Theodore Caplow, *The Sociology of Work* (University of Minnesota Press, 1954), p. 216.

15. City College of New York, *Faculty Senate News* (Faculty Senate, 1970), p. 2.

16. *Ibid.*, p. 8.

17. A number of other colleges and universities have been moving toward open admissions. Bowdoin College, for example, recently eliminated College Board scores as an entrance requirement. Richard M. Moll, the director of admissions, explains that "there is a widespread feeling and convincing evidence today that standardized aptitude and achievement tests cannot escape cultural bias and that they thereby work in favor of the more advantaged elements of our society, while handicapping others." *The Chronicle of Higher Education*, Feb. 2, 1970, p. 1.

18. Sexton, *The American School*, p. 54.

19. Harrington, *Toward a Democratic Left*, pp. 70–71.

20. Kingsley Widmer, "California: Why Colleges Blew

Up," *The Nation,* Feb. 24, 1969, pp. 237–241.

21. Healy, *loc. cit.,* p. 69.

22. *Ibid.,* p. 68. Copyright 1969 by Saturday Review, Inc. Reprinted by permission of author and publisher.

23. For a discussion of the blacks' revolution of rising expectations in specific contexts, see G. Louis Heath, "Corrupt East St. Louis: Laboratory for Black Revolution," *The Progressive,* October, 1970, pp. 24–27; "Ghost Town Vigilantes: The Racial Pallor of Cairo," *The Nation,* Dec. 22, 1969, pp. 692–695; and "Ghost Town," *The Nation,* May 24, 1971, pp. 644–645.

24. Christopher Jencks and David Riesman, *The Academic Revolution* (Doubleday & Company, Inc., 1969), p. 11.

25. *Ibid.,* p. 147. Copyright 1969 Doubleday & Company, Inc. Reprinted by permission of author and publisher.

26. Ivar Berg, *Education and Jobs: The Great Training Robbery* (Frederick A. Praeger, Inc., Publishers, 1970).

27. Ivan Illich proposes a radical "de-schooling" of society in favor of self-educating, self-authenticating inquiry into problems of vital concern to learners. See his "Why We Must Abolish Schooling," *The New York Review of Books,* July 2, 1970, pp. 9–15, and "The False Ideology of Schooling," *Saturday Review,* Oct. 17, 1970, pp. 56–58, 68–72. For a free copy of *Alternatives in Education,* the program Mr. Illich proposes, write CIDOC, APDO 479, Cuernavaca, Mor, Mexico.

28. Burton Clark, "The 'Cooling-Out' Function in Higher Education," *The American Journal of Sociology,* Vol. LXV (May, 1960), p. 569.

29. Prof. David C. Epperson has constructed a model for inquiry-oriented experiences within a system founded upon equal educational credits (tuition vouchers). His scheme financially frees learners to select their own learning experiences on the basis of interest alone, contracting voluntarily with other learners to participate in cooperative inquiry. The

learners, including the "master learners" (previously known as "teachers"), control the learning agenda as partners and evaluate it according to the quality of the total experience, not individual achievement. The authority for the educational experience resides in the learner. See David C. Epperson, "University Faculty and Cultural Pluralism: An Alternative to Traditional Myth-making Rituals," mimeographed (Northwestern University: Center for Urban Affairs, 1970).

30. Eliezer Krumbein, "Why Independent Schools?" mimeographed (University of Illinois: Chicago Circle, 1970), pp. 2–7.

31. Illich, "The False Ideology of Schooling," pp. 56–58, 68.

9

De Facto Segregation in a California City *

The issue of integration in the public schools has deeply polarized the San Francisco Bay Area community of Richmond. Financial resources, desperately needed for competitive faculty salaries and quality education, are not being adequately provided. Largely because of racial friction, the community's support of education has become so limited that the 165,000-member California Teachers Association has imposed sanctions upon the Richmond Unified School District.

The district's tax rate is one of the lowest in the state. Four efforts to increase the tax rate since 1952 have failed. The Association of Richmond Educators, representing 1,300 of the districts 2,220 teachers, claims that "the political and civic leaders of this area have sabotaged the schools and mauled the futures of our young people." Serious community opposition to desegregation has produced the crisis. Although Richmond's school population is 38 percent black, few schools are significantly integrated. The achievement level of blacks is far below that of whites; the black schools are staffed,

* Originally appeared in *Integrated Education,* Vol. VIII, No. 1 (Jan.–Feb., 1970), pp. 3–10. Reprinted by permission.

equipped, and maintained at a substandard level; and, much of the white community is rigidly committed to maintaining the imbalance.

Racial tension is acute in Richmond. Many parents are fearful of having their children bused to black areas. Some have even expressed fear of bodily harm if they must attend school board meetings in "undesirable" areas. Hysteria on the desegregation issue has been apparent on radio and television call-in shows and at school board meetings. One of the pro-integration board members, Dr. Maurice Barusch, has been subjected to threats on his life by "neighborhood schools" advocates. "Just the other day," according to Barusch, "my 15-year-old boy answered the phone to hear a woman screaming obscenities into it before he hung up." Barusch has requested and received police protection.

Richmond mayor John Sheridan has initiated a dialogue with black spokesmen aimed at diminishing racial tensions and improving community relations. Participants in the exchange have agreed upon a five-point racial harmony program. The program includes proposals to have foot patrols, psychological testing of police recruits, hiring of black youths for a police job-training program, and meetings of officers with groups of hostile black youths. That such conversations are necessary is indicative of great community tension.

THE SANCTIONS PROGRAM

In September, 1968, the Association of Richmond Educators requested the California Teachers Association (CTA) Personnel Standards and Ethics Commission to study the school crisis. The ensuing report identified twenty areas of serious educational deficiency, concluding with the finding that "many of the prerequisites of a good education are not being provided." The report recommended that "concerted efforts toward resolving the problems of integration be continued until the goal of equal educational opportunities is realized for every child." A second investigation in January, 1969, by a special panel assembled by the Personnel Standards and Ethics Commission assessed efforts to correct the district's deficiencies. Noting the lack of progress since the first study, the Commission recommended the imposition of state sanctions upon the 44,000-pupil Richmond district.

The CTA and the Association of Richmond Educators have requested the 1.2 million-member National Education Association to expand the sanctions nationwide. The NEA Professional Rights and Responsibilities Commission and the NEA Executive Committee are considering the joint request. The CTA action marks the first time a major California urban system has been blacklisted. (Two rural districts were sanctioned in 1959 and 1962.) The impact of the sanctions is expected to nearly dry up the supply of teachers available to replace the estimated five hundred to six hundred who will leave the district this year. Under the sanctions program, CTA notifies all teachers in California that "unsatisfactory educational and teaching conditions" exist in Richmond. It requests college and other placement services throughout the nation to "warn all possible candidates that Richmond does not offer an acceptable level for professional service." It notifies business and industry that educational opportunities for youngsters in the community are substandard. The county coordinating council, representing sixteen CTA-NEA chapters with 5,649 members, has formally endorsed the sanctions. Telegrams offering full support have come from as far afield as Winston-Salem, North Carolina, and Tampa, Florida.

LEGAL ASPECTS

The California State Board of Education has adopted what is probably the nation's first, concrete definition of racial imbalance. It defines segregation as existing whenever the racial composition of a single school deviates by more than fifteen percentage points from the total school district's racial composition. (One unofficial guideline used previously in various states held that segregation existed if a school had more than 60 percent minority students.) Thus, a school in the Richmond district, which has a 38 percent Negro student population, would be considered racially imbalanced if it had less than 23 percent or more than 53 percent Negro students. The Berkeley public schools, six miles away, satisfy the new guideline completely: the composition of each class is consistent with the city's racial statistics—51 percent white, 40 percent Negro, 9 percent Oriental. This integration has required the two-way busing of some 9,000 children in seventeen elementary schools. (The junior high schools were integrated in 1964 and there is only one high school.) The new school policy is incorporated as an amendment to the State Administrative Code, which has the force of law. (See "Race and Schools," *Integrated Education,* May–June, 1969, pp. 36–37, for text of the amendment.) The state's commissioner on equal opportunities in education is empowered to seek compliance from imbalanced school districts. *De facto* segregation has been alleged against several school districts in the state, including the San Francisco, Los Angeles, and Pasadena districts. The American Civil Liberties Union has a suit in Los Angeles Court asserting that the huge Los Angeles school system is doing too little to eliminate *de facto* segregation among its students. (See "Race and Schools," *Integrated Education,* July–Aug., 1969, p. 69.)

The leading California case on the subject of racial imbalance in the public schools is the 1963 decision of Jackson vs. Pasadena City School District. Chief Justice Gibson, writing an opinion concurred in by all members of the California Supreme Court, said in part:

> Residential segregation is in itself an evil which tends to frustrate the youth in the area and to cause anti-social attitudes and behavior. Where such segregation exists, it is not enough for a school board to refrain from affirmative discriminatory conduct. . . . The right to an equal opportunity for education and the harmful consequences of segregation require that school boards take steps insofar as reasonably feasible to alleviate racial imbalance in the schools, regardless of its cause.

The courts earlier ruled that the Richmond school administration must implement a three-year integration plan. There is currently some one-way busing of minority students into predominantly white schools within the Richmond Unified School District. The program costs $148,000, of which the Federal Government pays 30 percent through various grants under Title I of the Elementary and Secondary Education Act. Preparation was made last spring to implement the three-year integration plan, which requires two-way busing. Some $39,000 in Title VI grants were available for the in-service training of teachers to aid with the execution of the plan. Staff meetings were held to determine how to communicate plans to the general public. The district's human relations consultant also organized community committees to help effect integration plans as smoothly as possible.

THE POLITICAL BATTLE IN RICHMOND

Discord in the community recently produced an intense political climate. Polarization occurred about the political forces represented on the board of education, namely, integrationist and segregationist. Goy Fuller and Virgil Gay represented the segregationist forces. They voted against two-way busing, human relations institutes for youth, and tax increases for education. They stressed the preferability of the "open enrollment" plan, the great expense and inconvenience of busing, the possibility of Government control, and the threat to the security of children (in context, meaning white children). Their support came from such groups as Citizens for Neighborhood Schools and Save Our Schools. Mrs. Margaret Berry, Mrs. Betty Stiles, and Dr. Maurice Barusch constituted the five-member board's integrationist majority. They advocated integration, a tax hike for quality education, and an improved teacher salary schedule. (The Richmond schedule is the lowest of the eighteen largest districts in the state.) They received the support of such groups as Citizens for Excellence in Education (CEE), Legal Action Committee for Equal Schools (LACES), and the Richmond Advisory Committee on *De Facto* Segregation.

The hostility between the segregationist minority and

the integrationist majority was apparent at school board meetings. The segregationists frequently attacked the integrationists orally. Shouts from the audience were directed at both factions. Physical violence did not erupt in the audience, as it had over the same issue at a San Francisco board meeting, but disorder threatened on a number of occasions. For example, the segregationist minority opposed placing a measure for a tax increase on the ballot this year essentially because some of the money was required by court decision for two-way busing. Since Mrs. Berry was ill in a Los Angeles hospital, the Barusch-Stiles vote for submitting the proposal to the voters was insufficient. Mrs. Berry was flown to Richmond and brought by ambulance to the board meeting. As she was lifted from the ambulance to attend the meeting to cast the deciding vote, anti-integrationist parents gathered in a crowd, crying, "Drop her." Shouting and fist-shaking were a part of every board meeting. With such a high level of dissension, real communication was severely inhibited.

Political activity in Richmond intensified during campaigning for the school board election held April 15, 1969. One three-man ticket was supported by the United School Parents and Committee for Neighborhood Schools. Their platform called for no "forcible two-way busing," promoting better discipline in the schools, and a tax increase. Their billboard campaign signs read: "Money for schools . . . not busing." Candidate William Jageman did "not want anyone to say we're segregationists. I oppose two-way busing against the parents' consent. . . . Big Brother government is usurping parental authority." Another coalition of three supported the tax hike, increasing the school board to seven members, and integration through two-way busing. Rev. James Smith, the black member of the coalition, espoused the view that "separation will destroy our schools, our community, and our society." A total of fifteen candidates entered the race: ten integrationists against five segregationists.

The expressions of opinion in the communities served by the school district were diverse and indicative of the tension within the community, converging upon the issues of integration, busing, a tax increase, and teachers' sanctions. The *Richmond Independent* supported a tax increase and urged community compliance with the court order on integration. The *El Sobrante Herald* opposes public education as a form of social welfare. For the *Herald,* integration of the schools was patently absurd. Dr. L. C. Keating of Save Our Schools warned that the Berry-Stiles-Barusch master plan is "to create educational parks down the spine of the district, which would require busing virtually every student." Superintendent of schools Dr. D. E. Widel stated that "there is a chance that the schools may not open in September." The California Teachers Association and the Association of Richmond Educators predicted that if there is no tax increase, the ultimate effect would be disastrous for the area's business climate, property values, and community morale. The Citizens Committee on Equal Educational Opportunities concluded that the "only real way to solve the segregation problem is by two-way busing." The American Federation of Teachers, two hundred strong in Richmond, considered a possible strike, if the tax increase proposal were not approved.

The conservative five-member school board elected in April took the busing issue to court during the summer, securing a one-year delay in implementation of the two-

way busing plan so that it might try an "open enrollment" plan. The presiding judge indicated that the plan
would probably not work but granted a temporary sus-
pension of the planned three-year, two-way busing program for achieving integration, advising the board members that they would have to return to the involuntary
busing plan if they did not make substantial progress toward integration in the coming year using the voluntary
plan. To date, only two hundred students have signed up
to be voluntarily bused to other schools. And many are
white students seeking to move from one racially imbalanced school to an even more racially imbalanced one.

The Richmond schools opened this fall in demoralized
fashion, a situation which has allowed for a type of
apathetic peace. A considerable number of the best
teachers have left for better jobs. Their replacements are
basically part-time substitutes, provisionally credentialed
teachers, and lesser qualified graduates of colleges of
education, who found it expedient to ignore the sanctions imposed upon the district. The Richmond district is
only able to offer a full educational program because an
emergency tax measure passed during the summer. A
group of concerned citizens hurriedly, but effectively,
organized to secure approval of a moderate tax increase.
The measure, approved by a narrow margin, increases
the tax rate by $1.50. The defeated April 15th proposal,
regarded by the CTA as seriously inadequate, but apparently viewed as excessive by the voters, asked for a
$2.50 increase. So, Richmond has passed its first tax in-
crease in seventeen years, not so much to provide quality
education for all but to avoid providing no education at
all.

CONCLUSION

The higher tax proposal failed and a totally segregationist school board was elected. The need for two-way busing to achieve integration had apparently elicited considerable backlash in Richmond's white community. The political dialogue had not been concerned with the quality of education for all children, but rather with the peripheral issue of busing, which is really the issue of race. The community was generally unaware of the successful programs and research literature pointing to the interdependence of integration and quality education. They did not know or wished to ignore the fact that integration does not impede white students' achievements and often helps blacks. They did not regard busing as a method of effectively dealing with racism. Polemics focused upon the "neighborhood schools" question. Although a few liberals stressed that whites and blacks learn best *together*, argumentation generally gravitated toward emotionally loaded symbols, aborting rational discussion of the community's educational problems. The consequence is that adequate educational programs for all students have not been provided. Even passage of the higher tax increase proposal, albeit a welcome relief from financial pressures, would have only brought the Richmond district into parity with a few poorly financed districts in the state. The basic problem in Richmond is not money but impoverished human relations.

10

The Control Identities
of Negro and White Students
in a California City *

Control identity is the degree to which an individual
feels he possesses self-determination, particularly in
areas highly apposite to success as socially defined.[1] The
two most important areas for the highly valued socioeconomic success in American society are occupation
and education. The individual's perception of his control
over these two career lines, and his total sense of destiny
control, constitute the most significant component of
American control identity. Social class, with its accom-
panying gradations in income, personality traits, and living conditions, is an important mediating variable,[2] but
previous research demonstrates the present independent
significance of education and occupation.

Inquiry into control identity is particularly significant
in urban areas. It is in the city, particularly the inner
city, that the vaunted traditional American values of in-
dividualism, self-reliance, and self-fulfillment have been
encroached upon most by apathy, isolation, and fatalism.
In fact, the process of alienation in the cities has become

* Originally appeared in *Journal of Secondary Education,* Vol.
45, No. 5 (May, 1970), pp. 209–213. Reprinted by permission.

a major crisis of our predominantly urban civilization. Although both suburb and inner city have been affected by the disintegration of traditional consensual meaning in the megalopolis, the poor, the colored, the old, and the infirm—disproportionately ghetto residents—have suffered most under the impact of urbanization. This simplification of complicated historical process is not to say that rural life is particularly eufunctional for these groups, but some historians and social scientists will argue that it is more tolerable. The high suburbanite usage of barbiturates and amphetamines provides an indicator of life satisfaction in the high income areas. The city, streaked with socioeconomic-ethnic strata, has not been exceedingly uplifting for any group. The very structure of the metropolis has militated against a life-oriented culture there. The emphasis has been upon fitting men into the production, transportation, and distribution process of the city, where the individual becomes a "systems component" for externalized goals, toward which he labors rather than works. The most alienated (the unemployed) do not even enjoy the feeling of performing a limited function. The feeling of lack of destiny control (a negative control identity) among the ghetto poor is only a pronounced reaction to the urban dialectic which also affects the suburban well-to-do.

This paper compares the occupational and general aspects of control identity among Negro and white students in a California city. The qualitative analysis presented is based upon data employed in a broader study by the writer. The data are a product of the Richmond Youth Project at the University of California at Berkeley.[3] The Richmond Youth Project staff administered survey questionnaires to students in the eleven public junior and senior high schools of Western Contra Costa County during the spring of 1965. Western Contra Costa County is located in the East Bay area of the San Francisco Bay region. It is contiguous with Berkeley in the south, San Francisco Bay in the west, San Pablo Bay in the north, and a chain of hills in the east. The professionals and executives of the East Bay reside in the hills; the manual worker and Negro populations dwell in the flatland region between the hills and the bay. The major city in the western county is Richmond, an industrial community of 100,000.[4]

The sample for the study was drawn from Western Contra Costa County's public junior and senior high school student population of 17,500 in the fall of 1964.[5] This population was stratified by school, grade, race, and sex. Disproportionate random samples were drawn from each of 130 populated substrata. If a substratum were sufficiently large to generate a sample of at least 25 students, then 30 percent of non-Negro boys, 12 percent of non-Negro girls, 85 percent of Negro boys, and 60 percent of Negro girls were selected. If 25 students could not be secured from a stratum with these sampling fractions, the fraction was increased to 1.0, thereby including all students in the category. Except for those cases where the entire population of a stratum was drawn, simple random samples were drawn within each stratum. This methodology generated a stratified probability sample of 5,545 students. A complete set of data was secured for 73.5 percent of the original sample. The 4,077 completed questionnaires distribute into race-sex categories as follows: Negro boys, 1,001; white boys, 1,588; Negro girls, 813; and, white girls, 675.

The sampling error is calculated by a comparison of

the distribution of a variable in the population with the same measure in the sample—in this case, an indicator of achievement, namely, Differential Aptitude Test scores. The mean of the raw scores for the total population of 11,881 students having officially recorded scores on the Verbal Reasoning section of the DAT is 15.91 with a standard deviation of 9.35. The estimate of the population mean based upon a drawn sample of 5,545 is 15.73. This figure is less than .02 of a standard deviation below the population mean of 15.91. Hence, sampling error is negligible. Estimates of other population parameters corroborate this inference.

Nonresponse bias is slightly greater than sampling error. The estimate of the population mean for the DAT Verbal Reasoning Test, derived from the final sample of 4,077 cases, is 16.63. This figure is .077 standard deviation from the population mean of 15.91. The estimate based on the originally drawn sample is only 0.02 standard deviation from the population mean. Nonresponse is, therefore, somewhat greater than random sampling error, but not really significant. An analysis of mean weighted average grades in English according to response categories confirms the finding. The credibility of the data is established.

Multivariable measures of occupational and general control identity were devised.[6] For example, seven variables were used as a construct for "Concern Over Vocational Identity," operationally referred to as "CVOID" in the project's systems terminology. The variables are: (1) Are you worried about knowing what your real interests are? (2) Are you worried about knowing what you will do after high school? (3) Are you worried about knowing what work you are best suited for? (4) Are you worried about deciding whether you should go to college? (5) Are you worried about how much ability you really have? (6) Are you worried about finding out how you can learn a trade? and (7) Are you worried about being able to find a job after you get out of school? The correlations among these items range from .213 to .601 for all race-sex categories. These are sufficient to establish factorially the cluster quality of the measures.

Two items measured the general component of control identity: (1) What is going to happen to me will happen no matter what I do and (2) A person should live for today and let tomorrow take care of itself. The correlations are: Negro boys, .257; white boys, .312; Negro girls, .217; and, white girls, .400. Three variables provide an indicator for "Sense of Self-Control": (1) I have a lot of trouble controlling my temper; (2) I can't seem to stay out of trouble no matter how hard I try; and (3) I often have trouble deciding what are the right rules to follow. The correlations range from .210 to .272 for Negro boys, .226 to .250 for white boys, and are on a similar level of magnitude for girls. The items "I am not the person I pretend to be"; "I often feel that I would like to be someone else"; and "Things are all mixed up in my life" provide a measure of Identity Confusion. The correlations range from .251 to .400 for Negro boys, and .208 to .337 for white boys. The minima and maxima for girls are similar. The items "Planning is useless since one's plans hardly ever work out" and "There is no sense in looking ahead since no one knows what the future will be like" constitute an indicator of the concept "Future Time Orientation." The correlations are: Negro boys, .344; white boys, .260; Negro girls, .313; and, white girls, .259. The questionnaire items "Most people don't care what happens to you" and "Everyone in this world is out for himself" operationalize the concept of "Trust." Correlations are: Negro boys, .108; white boys, .218; Negro girls, .233; and, white girls, .261. The magnitude of the correlations for the several measures above establish statistically the integrity of the constructs.

Statistical analysis of control identity for Negro and white students demonstrates significant differences between the two groups, for both boys and girls. The Negro student feels he has less control over his ambience than the white student. He is more frustrated in developing a vocational identity, has a lesser feeling of self-control, experiences a greater sense of identity confusion and uncertainty as to what the future holds for him, and is more fatalistic and less trusting than his white counterpart. The Negro student has a negative control identity; the white student has a positive one. The Negro experiences existential frustration in his ambience; that is, there is poor articulation between present activity and the status for which he aspires. The disparity between deeply internalized, culturally sanctioned success norms and the paucity of the wherewithal to achieve those standards, generates the Negro's negative control identity. The realities of *de facto* school segregation, substandard housing, high unemployment, and self-discrimination remove most Negroes so far from the society's institutionalized channels of success that they despair; hence, they perceive themselves more as passives and inerts than dynamic actors establishing a new integrity, role, and self-definition. Simmel observes that "the deepest problems of modern life derive from the claim of the individual to preserve the autonomy and individuality of his existence in the face of overwhelming social forces of historical heritage, of external culture, and of the technique of life." [7] The urban Negro students of this study exemplify the atomization and sense of powerlessness to which Simmel alludes. A small percentage of white students also have negative control identities, but, statistically, there is a difference between whites and blacks *qua* groups.

The whites who have negative control identities often have many of the social characteristics that previous research has generally associated with Negro life-styles. They come from lower-income homes where the parents have low educational attainment; the families are large; the parents are much more authoritarian and physical than verbal and explicative in the treatment of their children and they do not socialize high achievement values; and, the father is a manual worker, and is generally dissatisfied with his job. This ambience can probably best be approximated in a term by Oscar Lewis' "culture of poverty." A product of that "culture" is the negative control identity of those who are so unfortunate as to be a part of it. A process of stigmatization, culminating in negative control identity, is central to the culture of poverty.

De facto segregation is an important correlate of Negro negative control identity in Richmond. Richmond's school-age population is 38 percent black, but few schools approximate this percentage in their enrollment. And it is in the imbalanced schools that the students are disproportionately characterized by negative control identities. The term "imbalanced" implies "segregation" in this paper. The California State Board of Education has defined segregation as existing whenever the racial composition of a single school deviates by more than 15 percent from the total school district's racial composition.

Segregation and control identity are integrally related. Coleman found that the student's sense of control of environment increased as the proportion of whites in the school increased.[8] Wilson determined that *de facto* segregation produced schools with "unequal moral climates" which affect the student's motivation.[9] There is abundant psychological and educational evidence on the damage suffered by all students, particularly black, who attend segregated schools. It is no surprise that Negro students in inferior, segregated schools should have negative control identities.

NOTES

1. For a related consideration of inner-city students' fatalism, nonutilitarianism, short-term hedonism, and existential frustration, cf. G. Louis Heath, "The Rebels of East Bay: A Study of Adolescent School Rebellion in the San Francisco Bay Area" (unpublished Ph.D. dissertation, University of California, Berkeley, 1969), especially Ch. III, "The Identity of the Rebel," pp. 34–65.

2. Cf., e.g., Richard A. Cloward and James A. Jones, "Social Class: Educational Attitudes and Participation," in *Education in Depressed Areas,* ed. by A. Harry Passow (Teachers College Press, Columbia University, 4th printing, 1965), pp. 190–216, and Martin Deutsch, "The Role of Social Class in Language Development and Cognition," *American Journal of Orthopsychiatry,* Vol. XXXV, No. 1 (January, 1965), pp. 78–88.

3. A National Institute of Mental Health grant (MH-0097) supported the Richmond Youth Project. The writer is indebted to Dr. Alan B. Wilson, director of the

project, for permission to analyze and report certain segments of the data. The writer's research has been supported by a United States Office of Education grant (OEG-9-8-001635-0082) and a generous allocation of University of California subsidized computer time.

4. Alan B. Wilson, "Western Contra Costa County Population, 1965: Demographic Characteristics" (Berkeley: Survey Research Center, University of California, 1966).

5. The description of the sample is based upon Alan B. Wilson, Travis Hirschi, and Glen Elder, "Technical Report No. 1: Secondary School Survey" (Berkeley: Survey Research Center, University of California, 1965), pp. 3–21.

6. "Explanation of Indices, Deck 6/8, High School Sample," Richmond Youth Project, mimeographed (Berkeley: Survey Research Center, Univeristy of California, June, 1967).

7. Georg Simmel, *The Sociology of Georg Simmel,* tr. by Kurt H. Wolff (The Free Press, 1950), p. 409.

8. James S. Coleman *et al., Equality of Educational Opportunity* (U.S. Government Printing Office, 1966), p. 323.

9. Alan B. Wilson, "Residential Segregation of Social Classes and Aspirations of High School Boys," *American Sociological Review,* 24:845 (Dec., 1959) and "Educational Consequences of Segregation in a California Community" (Berkeley: Survey Research Center, University of California, 1966).

11

Southern Illinois

The black demand for better education often occurs in a community situation where there are a number of serious problems. The scarcity of adequate housing and jobs, and discrimination in the courts and unions often provide the context for educational grievances. In short, educational deficiencies and inequities are inseparable from the total community situation. Nowhere does this seem to be more true than in southern Illinois, where poverty and racism guarantee that politically aware blacks will demand better treatment in every sphere, including education.

Cairo and East St. Louis are the two most outstanding examples of racially polarized communities in southern Illinois. Both communities face so many unsolved problems that their very security is threatened. The following essays describe the situations in both communities, setting the educational grievances and aspirations of blacks against the backdrop of the community tension and conflict from which they are inextricable.

A. GHOST TOWN VIGILANTES:
THE RACIAL PALLOR OF CAIRO *

Cairo, a town of 6,200, 45 percent black, stands at the confluence of the Ohio and Mississippi Rivers. This is the southernmost point of Illinois and in Cairo prejudice is often translated into action. Intense enmity between white and black has been a historical constant here; confrontation and violence have frequently cracked the veneer of community order, particularly since World War II. Recently, hostilities have escalated. Fire bombings and snipings are common occurrences, and several buildings have been burned to the ground (if a destroyed business has hired Negroes, the suspicion is that the arsonists were white). A few blacks have been wounded, and at least one has been killed. There are incessant threats, implicit or overt, mostly from whites. Considerable numbers of machine guns and other weapons have been sold to both blacks and whites.

Black militancy is the current spark to Cairo's traditional powder keg. The blacks, particularly the younger ones who have not been assimilated into the ante-bellum Southern mores (Cairo lies south of Richmond), are challenging established authority relationships, whereby whites proclaim decisions and "nigras" shuffle off to church to stifle their hatred of "the Man" by praying to the Lord. Blacks, organized in the United Front, are now assertively asking for a greater role in city government,

---

* Adapted from the author's articles "Ghost Town Vigilantes: The Racial Pallor of Cairo," *The Nation*, Dec. 22, 1969, and "Ghost Town," *The Nation*, May 24, 1971. Reprinted by permission. See also "Guerrilla War in Cairo," *The Nation*, Nov. 23, 1970.

more Negro policemen, and jobs in the businesses which they until recently patronized, but now boycott. They are defying white paternalism as fervidly as they once chopped cotton.

As late as the summer of 1966, Negroes in the three southern Illinois counties, Alexander, Pulaski, and Massac, were chained to low-paying cotton-chopping jobs by the seasonal withdrawal of welfare payments. Each spring the Alexander County office of the Illinois Public Aid Commission notified Cairo Negroes who received aid to dependent children that payments were to be terminated because seasonal labor was available. The labor was in the cotton fields of southern Illinois, southwestern Kentucky and southeastern Missouri, from May to September at 50 cents an hour. William H. Robinson, a black member of the Illinois Advisory Committee to the U.S. Commission on Civil Rights, reported in 1966: "There is evidence of collusion between the large farmers of the three states, the public aid department, and the Illinois State Employment Service to keep the Negroes in a form of slavery by paying them slave wages. When workers return to welfare rolls after the cotton-picking season, they are put on general assistance which pays less than regular welfare payments." The Illinois Advisory Committee's findings stimulated a larger investigation and the practice has been abolished.

The white community has been unable to deal with the new black militancy on any rational level. Their major response, following a black civil disturbance in July, 1967, has been to organize a white vigilante group, the White Hats, allegedly "to protect our families, our homes, and our property," but actually to defend ingrained values and practices against the onslaught of the new movement. The present state's attorney for Alexander County, Peyton Berbling, was one of the organizers and even served as an officer. The group is now defunct, but the fact that a man who was once an agent of a terrorist organization could become the foremost representative of the law in Cairo says much about the quality of its justice. The White Hats armed six hundred citizens, and drilled conspicuously in the downtown park, wearing white pith helmets. They were deputized as sheriff's deputies and deputy coroners. Cairo businessman Philip D. Marsden once claimed, "I could get my dog deputized in this town." The White Hats periodically participated in target practice and crisis alerts.

The White Hats disbanded last spring under pressure from the state government, particularly from Lt. Gov. Paul Simon. The Apprehension of Horse Thieves and Other Felons Act, the legislation granting legal status to vigilante groups, was repealed at the same time. But a new group, United Citizens for Community Action (UCCA), has sprung up, and the Negro community views it as the same thing. One can even hear Negro children near the all-black Pyramid Courts housing project jumping rope and singing: "Where have all the White Hats gone? Not far away. Where have all the White Hats gone? They have gone underground to the UCCA."

The United Citizens practice a modern-day vigilantism. Equipped with two-way radios, they cruise the Negro district at night, sometimes with shotguns and rifles protruding from car windows. Both blacks and whites monitor civilian band radio in the evenings. (Preston Ewing, Jr., president of the local NAACP chapter, was until recently a radio and TV repair shop owner.) The messages remind one of the tactics of war-fare: "We're close to Niggertown now. The guns are in the back. Our station will be about 100 yards behind Niggertown." "O.K., I'm coming down Walnut now. I'm staying here on this side of the tracks, so if any make any move out of Niggertown, I can handle it." Other conversation focuses upon contingency tactics: "We can roll a string of boxcars in behind Pyramid Courts for cover, if we need 'em. Cuz the city cut down all the brush between the tracks and the Courts, there won't be no cover outside. We can pin 'em down inside." (On one occasion the blacks of Pyramid Courts cornered a guerrilla band of whites on a nearby levee.) This sort of dialogue is not unusual on citizen band radio in Cairo.

The black community organized the United Front in response to the vigilante threat. It also is armed, but it has sought to de-emphasize weapons, realizing that it would be the weaker side in any showdown. Thus, when an AWOL Cairo Negro soldier mysteriously "hung himself" in the local jail and an elderly black man was beaten to death, the blacks didn't make major issues of their suspicions, fearing a mass reprisal upon Pyramid Courts, residence for 2,000 of Cairo's 3,800 Negroes. Instead, the United Front has decided that the way to improve the Negro's position in the town is to wield as much economic power as possible. Accordingly, it declared a boycott of white business. It has been honored by all the blacks, who now buy at a black cooperative store established just north of Cairo or go thirty-eight miles to Cape Girardeau, Missouri. For some white merchants business has dropped by two thirds. "Hell," griped a motel owner, "I'd be out of business if it weren't for the state police and newsmen staying here. I'm losing a lot of money." A real estate man claimed he had sold only two houses since last January. "Me and my family, we're moving to Florida. It's got to be better there. My God, what do they want? They're on aid. They don't work." "I'm losing $150 a day," complained another businessman. "I'm a small businessman and that's too much to lose."

Refusal to patronize local business works a drastic effect upon Cairo, which is in a depression. Of eighty-six Illinois communities with populations ranging from 5,000 to 10,000, Cairo ranks first in family units earning less than $3,000 a year, the income level defined by the federal government as the minimum for subsistence. Some 44 percent of Cairo's families are below it. Cairo is second among the eighty-six towns in substandard housing: 45.8 percent of all families reside in such dwellings. Since 1960 only nine new houses have been built and more than two hundred have been torn down. There has been no public housing construction since 1927. Cairo is third in unemployment with a 9.4 percent rate. For blacks, the rate is twice as high and runs to 20 percent for the Negro males. Cairo is part of the Alexander-Pulaski Counties' depressed area, where Senator Mc-Govern's Select Committee on Nutrition and Human Needs found considerable hunger and malnutrition. Cairo and Alexander County rate at or near the top for Illinois in high school dropouts, premature births, infant mortality, disease, aid to dependent children, and old age pensions.

Part of Cairo's problem is a great loss of population; it has shrunk to one third of its 1920 figure. Those who leave are disproportionately the young, the potential leadership, which Cairo desperately needs if it is not to become a ghost town. Many whites display bumper stickers proclaiming "Cairo—Love It or Leave It." The young, black and white, have taken the bitter advice, emigrating to St. Louis and Chicago, abandoning Cairo to become "an ugly sepulchre, a grave uncheered by any gleam of promise," as Charles Dickens described it during his visit in 1842.

The tax base has diminished with the population decline, but the percentage of the population on welfare has not—in fact, it has increased. The miniscule population influx has been composed primarily of poor whites from Kentucky, Missouri, and Tennessee, who contribute little to the tax base. They compete with blacks for low-paying jobs; many have become resentful welfare recipients. Their presence heightens racial tension.

Father Gerald Montroy, since 1968 representative in Cairo of the Belleville, Illinois, Catholic Diocese (all of southern Illinois), referred to by Cairo whites as the "white nigger," and Rev. Charles Koen, a black leader of the United Front, have advised the state government that major violence lurks just below the ruffled surface. (The Reverend Koen was a controversial leader of the Black Liberators in St. Louis and East St. Louis in 1967 and 1968. The press has referred to him as an "extreme militant.") They have requested Governor Ogilvie to intervene with a long-term scheme for peace, rather than to continue treating the symptoms of basic problems as though they were isolated emergencies. They have even asked the Governor to declare Cairo a disaster area, but Ogilvie thought that unnecessary.

However, when the Cairo merchants began to feel the pinch of the boycott (six had liens on their businesses), President Nixon declared the part of southern Illinois which includes Cairo an economic disaster area, thereby making federal small business loans easily obtainable. This action, whether or not so intended, effectively undercuts the boycott.

The Governor has dispatched the Illinois National Guard to Cairo on two occasions, but only a temporary cessation of hostilities has been achieved. He has looked the other way throughout much of the trouble. Lt. Gov. Paul Simon has evinced more concern; he has visited Cairo, and has offered to serve as negotiator. But the United Citizens will have no truck with "outside interference" and "emotional sensationalism" on the part of politicians. The United Front, on the other hand, insists that the Governor or Lieutenant Governor act as negotiator in talks designed to end hostilities. To satisfy Negro demands after the disruptions in the summer of 1967, the white leadership made a "good faith" agreement; but it later reneged and destroyed any trust that may have existed between blacks and whites. Now the Front wants a binding agreement, signed by the parties to the dispute and by a high-ranking state official, preferably the Governor.

Cairo blacks have suffered numerous frustrations in their attempts to secure access to places of public accommodation. They sought to integrate the city swimming pool in 1962, gaining entry by force. After three weeks of unwilling integration (actually a series of sit-ins, demonstrations, cracked heads, and arrests), the city officials closed the pool, saying it was not making enough money, and later selling it to a private concern for one dollar. Today the pool remains closed.

The blacks also attempted in 1962 to integrate a skating rink, owned by Billy Thistlewood, then a member of the local police force. Thistlewood furnished local whites with clubs and chains to repel the intrusion. In 1967, Negro leaders asked that they be permitted to convert into a youth and community center a chicken processing plant that had folded. The city contended that it wanted to keep the factory available for new industry, but the building, after more than two years, stands vacant and unattended. Even the Cairo Little League is segregated; doctors persist in segregating their waiting rooms, and dentists refuse to treat Negro welfare recipients.

When the Cairo schools were integrated during the winter of 1967, four schools were abandoned (they were all-Negro ones; integration generally meant moving blacks into white schools). Black leaders asked the school board for use of the gymnasium in one of these abandoned premises as an activities center. The board refused the request, saying they had long-term plans for the property. "Fine," Negro leaders agreed, "let us use it until the plans are completed." The response was forthcoming within a few days when a bulldozer appeared on the scene and converted the gymnasium into a pile of rubble. City officials erected in its place two basketball goals, which stand at virtually the same locations as did the goals in the old gymnasium. Of the three remaining schools requested by black leaders, two were bulldozed to the ground (although white leaders claimed one of them was to become a medical center) and the other was sold to an all-white group to house a private school, Camelot Parochial. Camelot "serves the better, white children," according to school administrator, Rev. Larry Potts, the fundamentalist Baptist preacher who in 1968 clubbed to death with a baseball bat a seventy-two-year-old Negro, Marshall Morris. Potts was never indicted.

He contended that Morris was assaulting his wife in their home. He testified before an Illinois House of Representatives Special Investigating Committee that black militants put Morris up to the attack.

Potts believes the public schools have declined as a result of integration. "The first year after integration, it was chaos. A lot of parents pulled their children out of school then. Many of us felt we ought to give them another chance. The second year was even worse. So many parents just felt they couldn't send their children back again." Mrs. Freida Rose, who has enrolled her child at Camelot, but still retains her position as a board member for the public schools, noted: "We tried integration. But when the Negro children came into the schools, it was terrible. They wrote dirty words on the walls and used such terrible language that we just couldn't take it any more. It isn't that they're Negro. It's just that their morals are so atrocious. I guess they must learn it at home."

Black students in the Cairo public schools have been the target of systematic discrimination. Counselors advise Negro students to drop out of school. A frequent reason cited is that a student is too old for his grade level. Actually, many of the students encouraged to leave school are from families most active in the United Front. Teachers and administrators discourage Negro students from participating in the senior class trip, although all students raise funds for the trip. One student was expelled because he had allegedly been "too playful" with a white girl, and two were evicted from a school assembly for clenching their fists in the "Black Power" salute.

The virulent white racism of Cairo now threatens to collapse the town's public school system. Today, almost four hundred white students attend Camelot Parochial, ostensibly open to all, but the all-white student body and the pictures of former Alabama Governor George Wallace adorning the walls would lead one to infer otherwise. A few white students also commute to an all-white parochial school in Paducah, Kentucky, across the Ohio River. As an increasing number of students have opted for their children to attend Camelot or commute to Paducah, the public schools have become increasingly financially malnourished and racially blackened. Cairo's public school population declined from 1,632 in the 1968–1969 school year to 1,206 in 1969, a drop of 25 percent. During the same period, the percentage of white students declined from 50 percent to 26 percent. This caused a $243,000 decrease in state aid, which is based on average daily attendance. Since racial violence exploded in Cairo in March, 1969, the tax base has shrunk from $20.2 million to $17.3 million. Industries like Swift Packing and Singer have fled to more hospitable surroundings. The town's population dwindled from 8,400 to 6,200 in the same period. Pleading poverty with these data in March, 1971, the Cairo public school board claimed that it could no longer afford to operate a school system and would close down April 1.

But the Illinois Constitution requires the public schools to remain open. State Superintendent of Public Instruction Michael Bakalis halted closure, providing emergency funds. He dispatched a team of investigative lawyers to Cairo to ascertain why there was a financial crisis. The team was particularly interested in determining if public school money was being channeled into Camelot. A number of teachers in the public schools—interviewees who insist on protective anonymity—have charged that public school administrators are illegally channeling money and materials to Camelot Parochial. They have also charged that the school board members, all of whom send their children to Camelot, have no real interest in the public schools. Cairo's blacks believe that the white school board and county school officials are not concerned about keeping the predominantly black schools open. They feel the whites are trying to kill the school system as a reprisal for the black boycott that has devastated local white business. For example, the United Front, a black coalition, has often accused Grace Duff, superintendent of Alexander County Education Service Region, of not fully supporting the public schools. She recently fueled their suspicions by presenting a paper at the 76th annual convention of the North Central Association of Accreditation in Chicago entitled "Impact of Community Education on the Problem of Parent Discontent and Conflict Between Private School and Public School Views on Learning." In that paper, she effectively advocated private education as a *de facto* means of segregation.

Robert Simpson, Cairo school board president, claims that the public schools are so deeply in debt that they can only remain open three months beginning fall, 1971. And that even three months of operation will require that $400,000 be cut from the budget and half the staff be released.

"There is no easy way out for Cairo in this crisis," State Superintendent Bakalis has said. "It is going to require the same kind of belt-tightening that a family faces when it finds itself badly beyond the family budget. The public schools must remain open. The law demands that we provide a free public education to these youngsters, and I intend to see that the law is carried out."

Racial confrontation has fixed a ghostly pallor on Cairo. Although located on a rich alluvial fan at the confluence of two great arteries of transport and commerce, potentially greater than Chicago (and at one time larger' and more prosperous), the city is impoverished in 1971 because a rigid and paranoid social structure will not permit the rational use of resources, both human and physical.

The white leaders, believing God and the Bible to be on their side, would rather attack the boycott and the black militants than seek to eradicate the poverty and deprivation which victimize many of both races. A United Front resolution points out: "The real enemy of the poor people of Cairo, the black ones and the white ones, is the government (in Springfield and Cairo) which permits the poor to remain poor at the edge of an affluent society." The situation in Cairo is a classic one of wealthy elites, bound into a ruling clique, pitting one impoverished group against another. The white leaders know that if they can interpret every issue as a racial one, they will never lose an election (the population is 55 percent white). They fear any organization that cuts across the racial barrier. The Illinois Migrant Council met great opposition when it initiated its adult education program for underemployed seasonal farm workers. The assistant program director was badly beaten and the area coordinator was fired upon. The white leaders know that when impoverished whites and blacks study together, they are only one step from joint political action, and they fear collective militancy even more than black militancy. Black Power can be contained in Cairo because it is not sufficient to win political office, but the voices of the impoverished (at least half of the population), demanding change through the ballot box, could not be ignored.

A coalition of poor blacks and whites is not an immediate possibility. The polarization of the races in Cairo is, in fact, so great that it is difficult for black and white even to discuss their problems. White police Captain W. H. Thompson claims, "I have never seen so much hatred in my life as in this town." A truck driver snarls, "When the niggers learn that if they start cutting on a white man for no reason at all, they're going to get their heads blown off, they'll start leaving white people alone." A shopkeeper insists: "We got the dumbest goddam niggers in the country." The Reverend Potts, who regularly preaches on "Communism in Cairo," is the leading advocate of the "devil theory" espoused by most white citizens. He throws up his hands in disgust. "There's a criminal element in Cairo. There's a militant element that has come and gone back and forth from East St. Louis." A housewife confides: "We want to help the nigras, but these cruddy black 'Castro guerrillas' just keep on agitating. These things take time." This thinking in stereotypes, this imputing of the basest motives to a whole group, creates a sociological climate of intolerance. The most minor incident can set off violence.

The blacks in Cairo have refused to turn inward the antagonism they feel toward whites. There has been some militant preying upon moderate blacks who do not agree with the activist strategy, even one killing, but it has not been much, given the intensity of feelings. The *Cairo News,* published by the blacks, moralizes: "The one lesson we hope the White Hats have learned is that there is a new black man, woman, and child in Cairo. They all stand ten feet tall and they can smell a sick racist miles away and long before they can begin to deceive the blacks."

The blacks have sought full participation in civic life by initiating legal challenges to discriminatory practices. For example, the United Front challenged a proclamation, issued under the authority of a Cairo City Ordinance, banning picketing in the corporate limits. The Front won with the legal assistance of Robert Lansden, a lawyer and one of the few white liberals in Cairo, who took the case to federal court in Danville, Illinois. Lansden also handled cases for Cairo blacks in 1949 and 1952, winning on both occasions. For his efforts, his home has been fire-bombed and garbage has been strewn on his lawn. One neighbor, after suffering an accidental fire bombing of his porch, erected on his roof a neon arrow pointing toward Lansden's place. David Baldwin, president of the United Front, feels the boycott would be successful without picketing, but that the activity sustains in all blacks a sense of involvement that is essential to the black movement in Cairo.

Through the United Front, the blacks have discovered what it means to be a constructive agent of change (and when destructive, generally in self-defense). They no longer accept Cairo's archaic, plantation system of values. But the white community, isolated by its collective illusion about what blacks are like, has hypnotized itself into believing that the "niggers" really do not mean all those things about "Black Power" and "black dignity." How long this fantasy will last is difficult to say, but the violence will continue until it ends.

B. CORRUPT EAST ST. LOUIS:
LABORATORY FOR BLACK REVOLUTION *

White racism has become an increasingly ineffective instrument of oppression in the East St. Louis black community—70 percent of the city's population of 68,000—simply because the young militant leaders have persuaded many blacks that they were not born to perpetual deprivation. The black radicals have nurtured a psychological awakening that has burgeoned into a revolutionary transformation of values. The blacks of East St. Louis will no longer accept the myth of their inferiority. They are willing to take the steps necessary to win, or enforce the equality they believe is their birthright. This is their revolution.

East St. Louis has been historically a racially violent city. A riotous massacre of thirty-nine blacks, much in the style of the Russian pogroms of the nineteenth century, stained the city crimson in 1917. Other disturbances have rocked the community since then. The most recent ones occurred in August and September of 1967, at the same time that the smoke of racial conflagration hung over Newark and Detroit.

The young militants, receptive to the national Black Power Movement and indignant about the discovery of voting fraud (voting graveyards and vacant buildings) in a mayoral election that black candidate Elmo Bush lost, eagerly listened to Stokely Carmichael when he visited East St. Louis in March, 1967, and cheered H. Rap

---

* Originally appeared in *The Progressive,* October, 1970. Reprinted by permission.

Brown in September. On the eve of September 10, when Brown departed East St. Louis, serious rioting began. The blacks, even the "Toms," were united in their belief that the police catalyzed the riot. Indisputable evidence —newspaper reports and photographs—sustained the allegation that the police had attacked a peaceful assembly of blacks. A total holocaust was fortunately avoided; the disorder ended in three days without massive violence and destruction.

Following the riot, the black militants organized Black Culture, Inc., late in 1967 and the Black Economic Union early in 1968. Black Culture's essential purpose is to promote black solidarity and revolution. It stresses unifying the black community through the dissemination of Afro-American culture; it is primarily interested in cultural revolution. The Black Economic Union is an ethnic organization, established to countervail institutionalized white racism with collective Black Power and "drive the white man from our city." The specific aim is to wrest control of the exploited ghetto from absentee landlords and investors through the application of black economic power in such forms as selective buying and the establishment of cooperatives. The Union's ultimate strength resides in its militancy, the not so subtle threat that violence is justifiable given sufficient provocation.

Newspaper reports of police raids and racial violence pulse like adrenalin through the social veins of East St. Louis. Whites have set sales records with their gun purchases, inadvertently divulging their anxiety. The white city fathers responded to the 1967 summer violence by organizing a crime control commission. The blacks denounced the commission as a vigilante group, intended only to subvert the momentum of black militancy under the guise of maintaining "law and order." Their immediate response to the commission was Black Culture, Inc.

The drive to develop Black Power in East St. Louis has unified a diverse set of black gangs which have traditionally been rivals. The Black Egyptians, Black Liberators, Black Nationalists, and Imperial War Lords now cling together in an uneasy alliance, rather than constantly contending with one another. (The tendency to confederate does, however, occasionally become tenuous. For example, the Black Egyptians' recreation room was recently fire-bombed, probably by one of the other gangs.) These groups, menacing and potentially violent as they seem to whites, add a convincing edge to the black economic and cultural thrust. They have synthesized the late Malcolm X's nationalism and Stokely Carmichael's Black Power into a workable program of action directed toward economic self-determination and political militancy, and laced with the threat of violence.

Dick Gregory spoke with a group of East St. Louis black militants at McKendree College, twenty miles from St. Louis, just after the Black Economic Union was organized: "You cats have a hippier thing going for you in East St. Louis than we've got in Chicago. You can reach everyone down here." Gregory is basically correct. There is a substantial degree of solidarity and ethnic consciousness among the East St. Louis blacks. The black revolutionaries' objections to the Vietnam war have even stimulated (or intimidated) black soldiers home on leave to shun khakis for mufti. Five years ago most blacks on leave wore their uniforms with some feeling of distinction.

Black nationalism is fostered by the Experiment in

Higher Education at Southern Illinois University's East St. Louis branch. Katherine Dunham, famed Negro dancer-choreographer-ethnologist and director of the Performing Arts Training Center affiliated with the university, has injected an Afro-American cultural element into the program. The Experiment's students are 95 percent black; their instructors and counselors are predominantly black. The curriculum is fluid and open, virtually unstructured, and the students have responded by turning their interests to the avant-garde strains of contemporary black culture. This black "curriculum of concerns," purely Deweyan, is really an academic crucible for the diverse elements that now loosely embody the new black identity. The blacks act out their values and feelings to synthesize disparate cultural strands into an authentic black identity. They have immersed themselves in black history and radical philosophy.

They find much that they read in the revolutionaries' justification of revolution by colonially oppressed peoples in Latin-American and Algerian contexts to be particularly relevant to their plight. The Experiment in Higher Education is unquestionably playing a major role in producing the intellectual leadership for the black revolution in East St. Louis.

East St. Louis, reputed by several accounts to be one of the most corrupt cities in the nation, provides all the ingredients for sustaining a revolution. Police corruption and brutality, a high density of black poverty, union racial discrimination that keeps blacks from jobs, and inept government assure that the black revolution will continue.

In the fall of 1968 a Michigan State University study reported that the East St. Louis police department's performance was deficient at all levels. The report cited fourteen major problems. Then Police Commissioner Russell T. Bebee blasted the report because he felt it would be too expensive to make the recommended improvements. One of the reforms the report advised was the removal of Bebee, who insisted on ordering police to shoot first and ask questions later. He eventually resigned. The MSU study detailed several incidents of racist behavior by the police such as severe beatings and compulsive shootings of blacks, and the use of epithets like "boy," "nigger," "darky," and "spade."

The new Police Commissioner, Ross Randolph, Director of Public Safety under Illinois Governors Otto Kerner and Samuel Shapiro, has attempted to improve police performance and police-community relations. He has achieved some success, especially in disciplining his police, who have initiated a trumped-up lawsuit against him for "malfeasance." However, his recent order to fire upon suspicious persons who do not stop after a warning shot has greatly diminished his credibility among blacks, particularly since a white has not been killed in a pursuit for more than a decade. Rex Carr, a radical, local, white lawyer and chairman of the city's Human Relations Commission, who specializes in unpopular cases, is handling the police suit against Randolph. Nevertheless, Carr frankly admits that he finds "a great many of the police are crooks and brutal thugs."

Hunger and nutritional deficiencies constitute a serious problem for blacks in East St. Louis. "The need is so great it is indescribable," according to Will McGaughy, black president of the Metro-East Health Services Council. Dr. Rose Cohnberg, now with the University of Missouri at St. Louis, served until recently as medical consultant to the Illinois Department of Public Health Poverty Division in East St. Louis. She notes, her voice filled with emotion: "We had children come to us who were gut-aching hungry because they simply had had no food. And we had old people come for the very same reason. There is no food, so people don't feel well." The young black leaders have convinced many that an empty stomach calls for a revolution.

The black Director of Police-Community Relations, Otis Simpson, sociologically observes: "The absentee white landlords in Belleville, Washington Park, and other surrounding suburbs live in paranoid fear of the city they exploit, but it doesn't occur to them to relieve the human suffering. We need black control of this city. White city administrators have only produced corruption and racial polarization."

The initial impetus for the black revolution was the crescendo of rage which painfully stirred black consciousness in 1965 and 1966. The NAACP then waged a concerted battle to secure employment opportunities for blacks on government projects in the East St. Louis area. It disclosed, for example, that only 15 of 398 employees on four federally financed highway construction projects were black, and most of them were laborers. The 1964 Civil Rights Act theoretically promised equality of opportunity, but the prospect of economic betterment turned to dust when grasped; white racism prevailed save for token concessions. The construction unions proved a bastion of virulent racism and systematic discrimination. The contractors were conveniently fearful of race conflict on the job and interested primarily in profit as usual. As for the Federal Government, it seemed at the time either blithely unconcerned, or narcotized by bureaucratic inertia, save a few U.S. Department of Labor officials who abortively endeavored to initiate effective action against discrimination.

The Federal Government finally shouldered its legal and moral responsibility on July 1, 1968, freezing all highway construction funds in St. Clair and Madison Counties because of noncompliance with the equal opportunity requirement on such federally supported projects. The freeze continued almost two years, ending June 3, 1970. One gaped upward like a tourist at Stonehenge at the sight of concrete freeways ending abruptly in midair, providing a ludicrous drop-off for the imagined motorist. But the unfinished structures intended to connect St. Louis to suburbs beyond East St. Louis were not the ruins of an ancient culture: they were, of course, East St. Louis in a federal fund freeze. During this abbreviated Ice Age, the Government faulted the unions for racial discrimination and excessive construction costs (the two are related).

The thaw arrived when the Illinois Governor's Office of Human Resources submitted a modest plan for a black job-training program to the U.S. Department of Transportation. The Metro-East Labor Council, representing the blacks, and the Southern Illinois Builders Association have accepted the plan, but only two of the construction unions have approved it. This unsubstantial program promises no basic change. Black leader Elmo Bush, principal of all-black Lincoln High School, explains: "The freeze wouldn't have been possible without the new black awareness and commitment to react to discrimination in a sustained, organized way. The black community is becoming increasingly mature and refuses to tuck under to white paternalism and tokenism."

The freeze exacerbated racial tension, undercut rational leadership, and took a heavy economic toll on the two-county area where 37 percent of all families struggle on annual incomes under $3,000. Forty-five percent of the black families in East St. Louis live precariously below this level. This full-scale depression is due basically to the fact that 33 percent of the East St. Louis blacks are unemployed, 15 percent are employed only part time, and the remainder are generally working at poorly paid, semiskilled and unskilled jobs, primarily in local manufacturing and service industries. An increasing number of blacks are also being employed in the lower levels of the city bureaucracy, as janitors, clerks, and typists.

Gangster complicity in the East St. Louis unions reinforces racial discrimination and blatant profiteering. A 1969 Illinois Institute of Technology construction report, authorized by the city of East St. Louis and funded through the federal Model Cities program, charges that criminal activity and collusion in the unions are, in part, responsible for high construction costs and racial discrimination. Costs in East St. Louis exceed the national average by 25 percent, and are even 15 percent higher than in Chicago, where the building trades unions are also adamant obstacles to the amelioration of race relations. Alvin G. Fields, former white mayor of East St. Louis, concealed the IIT report two months, and released it only when the local *Metro-East Journal* publicized his suppression of the document. Fields attempted to rebut the findings: "I personally don't think much of this report. It talks about past history, not the present. There is no control by hoodlums, to my knowledge, of anything at the present time."

But the carefully researched IIT study is not merely

congruous with the past of East St. Louis, when the Shelton and Wortman gangs ran the city, and even a mayor was assassinated; it also seems to speak truthfully of the present. The colleagues of Frank "Buster" Wortman, leader of the reorganized Chicago Capone gang in down-state Illinois from 1942 until Wortman's death in 1966, now occupy lucrative and influential sinecures in the unions. The Mafia, solidly entrenched in St. Louis and Chicago, extorts security payments from the East St. Louis contractors. It guarantees Mafia operations by heavily influencing, according to *Time* magazine, fifteen Illinois state legislators.

The IIT report concludes: "Coercive activities seem to have instilled fear in nearly all those unfortunate enough to have dealt with the construction industry in East St. Louis. . . . Supervisory personnel have been beaten—killed in one case—and heavy equipment destroyed. . . . Craftsmen who wish to conscientiously work are intimidated. Threats are made upon their lives or the safety of their families and property. . . . Coercive acts, beatings, and killing occur on the construction projects." The evidence strongly supports the inference that organized crime is exerting a major influence in the East St. Louis construction unions.

The East St. Louis construction industry is a microcosm of the industry nationally: it is extremely backward. It has resisted the introduction of new materials and techniques and the training of sufficient numbers of skilled workers to satisfy demand. A tacit agreement exists among East St. Louis contractors, union leaders, and politicians to preserve the *status quo*. The unions maintain a tight clamp on the supply of skilled labor in order to inflate wages artificially. Thousands have been denied union membership so that commitments to friends and relatives might be discharged. The non-union workers, mostly blacks, are left no alternative but to do small jobs, such as the construction of single-family dwellings in the outlying suburbs and rural areas. If a shortage of a particular skill arises, the unions bring in white workers from other areas rather than train blacks. Black independent contractors have been squeezed out of the market, often by violence, particularly the bombing of their equipment. This further depresses black employment prospects.

The East St. Louis construction industry, like the industry nationally, is capable of a complete technological revolution that could swiftly resolve the city's chronic housing shortage and contribute handsomely to satisfying the rising expectations of blacks. The modular system of construction allows segments of apartments and houses to be built on a factory assembly line, using all-steel wall systems, studs, and frames; the segments are then assembled on the housing site. On one experimental East St. Louis project where modular units were used (FHA would not insure the loan), a four-unit prototype was erected and ready for occupancy in approximately four hours.

The unions fear that modular construction is a threat to their prerogatives and the union movement itself. It is not really a threat, however, if the unions would but rationalize their organizational structure. The unions could rapidly train blacks for semiskilled prefab and modular work. The East St. Louis blacks, now thinking seriously about separate unions (a most basic threat to organized labor), would, in this fashion, soon strengthen the construction unions; they would be beneficially co-opted whereas at present they are isolated and national-istic, a constant concern. By utilizing prefab, modular, and other new construction technologies, the unions could reduce building costs, expand their work force (especially blacks, although initially at semiskilled lev-els), and because of huge unfulfilled construction needs still sustain their high wage rates. Such a policy would render a great service to improving East St. Louis race relations and meeting regional housing needs. Yet the unions will have no truck with reform.

The key issue today in the struggle between blacks and unions is the matter of who shall control the ap-prenticeship and training programs. The unions insist on directing the programs, which to date have included few blacks. By severely rationing admissions to the programs, the unions have won impressive wage scales and a lucrative array of job-related benefits. This ex-clusiveness has created, however, a world of "haves" and "have-nots," where a heavily disproportionate number of the "have-nots" are black. The East St. Louis construc-tion unionists, living in what must appear to blacks to be awesome opulence—the craftsmen are now making about nine dollars an hour—cannot see the merit of easing admission requirements for blacks. The white building tradesmen want no job competition. This ex-plains the findings of the research literature that rates unionists with policemen and Southern red-necks in the paranoid quality of their view of "niggers." The East St. Louis unionists can only think, "Bye, bye, blackbird," when they observe the blacks, moved by their new eth-nic consciousness, ask for some of the good things of

American life that can be had through union membership. They too easily forget (if they are old enough to
forget) that black workers want only what white workers sought in the 1930's: more.

The U.S. Department of Labor, sponsor of most federal manpower programs in East St. Louis, is loaded
with programs which train people for nonexistent jobs
in such areas as building maintenance and die casting.
Poor blacks have criticized the system of training that
circulates them from one project to another. They are
cynical about promises of employment after a year or
two of training that leads only to another such program.
The programs are really designed to channel blacks into
menial jobs, avoiding a confrontation with institutionalized discrimination, if the programs are for anything
more than pretense at all. One of the most controversial
projects trains gas station attendants. The black community, wanting upwardly mobile education, has ob-
jected to the denigrating curriculum that assumes that
pumping gas is the apex of the black man's aspirations.

The militants' emetic for the persistent brutality,
deprivation, and discrimination the East St. Louis black
community has nauseously absorbed so long for want of
a remedy is "self-defensive retaliation," whether economic, cultural, or military. East St. Louis is a testing
ground for revolutionary strategies. The militants have
touched a responsive chord in the black "silent majority."
The city is small enough and black enough for the militant leaders eventually to take control. The purchase of
apathetic black votes for five dollars is on the wane.
Absentee landlords are gradually liquidating their property assets and white residents, pursued by phantasms of

"Black Panther types," are fleeing the city on the vaulting, concrete freeways of callous unconcern that city planners have built for them to immolate psychologically the reality of black despair below.

A group of East St. Louis liberals, responding to their own fear and guilt and a sense of moral urgency, arranged to meet with the black revolutionary leadership to initiate a plan to obviate race warfare. One dashiki-garbed black, fingering a carved ebony fist hanging about his neck, aptly expressed the revolutionaries' intractability in an aggressive rebuff of one of the liberals: "The only way you can help us is by buying guns 'cuz you can get 'em easier than we can. Get us some guns and then get out of the way." This assertion is not solely cathartic. The police periodically confiscate (sometimes without a warrant) arms and ammunition caches, including dynamite and hand grenades, and occasionally what they have referred to as "plans of terrorism." (The War Lords employ the term "self-defense programs.") The black revolutionaries have used the dynamite and hand grenades. They are willing, if pressed, to wage a defensive war.

The late, great Willie Howard once said in a classic vaudeville skit, "Comes the revolution and we'll all live in penthouses and eat strawberries and cream." Although the blacks of East St. Louis are anxious for the millennium of penthouses, strawberries, and cream, they would prefer to achieve the revolution nonviolently, despite some of their affected rhetoric. However, if white racism does not abate so that blacks can find decent jobs, and conventional politics are ineffective in ousting corrupt white and black officials, the black revolutionaries are willing to employ more direct methods. The worst of all possible worlds in East St. Louis would be the head-on collision of uncompromising white hostility and angry black militancy. No sane and democratic resource should be left untried to avoid this collision and its explosive consequences before it is too late.

12

Berkeley

A. BERKELEY'S
EDUCATIONAL OPPORTUNITY PROGRAM *

The black demand for a place in American educational institutions has compelled a response that has been in part altruistic, in part self-interested. Many colleges and universities have acted upon a new definition of their social responsibility by providing financial and tutorial assistance to black learners. Nowhere has this endeavor been more committed and successful, according to *The Southern Education Report,* than at the University of California at Berkeley.

The salience of higher education to socioeconomic success points to the urgency of accommodating increasing numbers of disadvantaged youths in higher education. Education for the disadvantaged, who are disproportionately minority group members, moves the society closer to a fully rational use of human resources and

* Originally published by ERIC Information Retrieval Center on the Disadvantaged, Teachers College, Columbia University. ERIC Document Reproduction Service # ED 041986. Reprinted by permission.

provides legitimate channels to success. Educating the disadvantaged requires, however, special programs. Due to deficiencies in his educational experience, the disadvantaged student needs an intensive program of tutorial and financial aid to succeed in college. He requires a program of educational guidance.

The Berkeley campus of the University of California has responded to the challenge of the minority and low-income student in higher education. It has initiated the Educational Opportunity Program (EOP) to recruit the disadvantaged and provide financial support, tutoring, and counseling. The regents established Projects for Educational Opportunity to provide awards to students from disadvantaged backgrounds. The purpose of the program is to "assist and motivate California high school students who are members of culturally disadvantaged groups and who have demonstrated intellectual promise."

RECRUITMENT

The risk applicant must submit three to five letters of recommendation from teachers and counselors and write a biographical statement, including his plans for the future. The EOP admissions committee reviews the applicant's pattern of grades and sometimes requests a personal interview if supplementary information is desirable. A special committee consisting of the EOP director, the admissions officer, and the chairman of the Faculty Committee on Admissions reviews each application. Each member votes for or against admission.

The admission standards are flexible enough to accommodate those who are academically deficient but promising. High school performance is not the only indicator

of a student's college potential. The exclusive use of such
a measure is an efficient means of screening out the
minority group and low-income student. The high, positive correlation between economic standing and academic
achievement has been well established. The American
Council on Education's 1959 Conference on the Disadvantaged concluded, not surprisingly, that the financially able student has greater opportunity to prepare for
college than the minority group student who is burdened
by disrupted family life and an inferior, inner-city education. Numerous subsequent studies have demonstrated
the same phenomenon.

A survey of the 75 high schools in the San Francisco
Bay Area demonstrates that virtually no minority students prepare for college. In one of the state's most
achieving high schools, for example, only 89 of 1,300
blacks in the tenth to twelfth grades enrolled in college
preparatory courses and had a C average or better. There
were only 12 blacks from that high school at Berkeley,
the largest contingent from any one school.

Most minority, college preparatory students are girls,
but few enter college. Of the small number of minority
boys who prepare for college, only a few will go on to
college. The attrition rate for both groups during college
is quite high. Lack of academic preparation and financial resources force many minority students out. The
blunt fact is that, with the exception of blacks at predominantly black colleges, few minority group persons
are graduating from college.

The university-wide Office of Relations with Schools
operates a major program to recruit disadvantaged students. Its representatives visit some 120 high schools with
sizable minority enrollments annually in an effort to

interest these students to undertake college preparatory programs. A similar program is operative in the junior colleges. The Office also works in 60 junior high schools with a 30 percent or more minority population to promote enrollment in college preparatory courses. In addition, constant communication is maintained with county departments of social welfare, the California State Employment Service, and local poverty programs such as the East Bay Skills Center and the San Francisco Mission District Poverty Office.

Regularly admitted Berkeley students are very much involved in the effort to aid the disadvantaged. They are particularly involved in the College Commitment Program, funded by the Rosenberg Foundation and sponsored by the Berkeley campus in coordination with other four-year institutions in the San Francisco Bay Area. This program places university students in local high schools as assistant counselors to work with minority and low-income youth. They provide precollege counseling, tutoring during and after school, and financial aid information. They also confer with students' families, outlining the possibilities and realities of a college career. Six schools have been involved in the College Commitment Program. It is now being expanded to include twenty-five high schools. It will eventually serve all Bay Area high schools.

Graduate students have recently been included in the Educational Opportunity Program. In 1967, 20 students were in the program; the 1968 figure was 75; the 1971 figure is 95. In developing the Educational Opportunity Program for graduate students, the university has endeavored to prepare disadvantaged persons for professional work, especially teaching, law, medicine, and dentistry. The Berkeley EOP has also begun to recruit graduate students from southern black colleges. Visits are made to the black colleges and students there are encouraged to participate in a junior year program at the university as well as graduate study. The assumption is that students who spend a junior year at Berkeley will seriously consider graduate work at the university. A number of students from Tuskegee Institute in Montgomery, Alabama, who have completed a two-year pre-forestry course, will attend a Berkeley summer camp and subsequently complete their studies in forestry at Berkeley. Educational Opportunity funds and a grant from the National Science Foundation pay the expenses of students recruited from black colleges.

A number of university departments recruit and aid minority and low-income students. For example, a special committee in the Berkeley School of Social Welfare has recruited black and Spanish surname students since 1964. It received recently a $258,000 Carnegie Corporation grant to increase further the department's minority enrollment. The Department of Mathematics has a program to provide financial and academic assistance for students who are inadequately prepared in mathematics. The Department of Education seeks minority students who wish to train as teaching professionals. Eight other departments are also involved in aiding the disadvantaged.

PROFILES OF RECRUITED STUDENTS

The Educational Opportunity Program serves a cross section of the disadvantaged. A sketch of a few former EOP students will indicate this diversity. A black woman with a school-age child entered the program as a junior college transfer. She maintained a B average at the university. Another mother enrolled at the university, later followed by her daughter. A sixty-year-old black woman was admitted. Two men over thirty-five enrolled. A black man matriculated at Berkeley only a few weeks after his release from San Quentin as a two-time offender. Two of his writings were recently accepted for publication. He told the EOP director that he finally felt that he had a purpose in life and an opportunity to achieve it. (Four other men from San Quentin subsequently applied to the university.) A twenty-seven-year-old American Indian, proficient in English, French, and Russian, came to the university without funds. He achieved a B plus average. A Mexican-American, twenty years old, entered the university following Navy service. Although not regularly admissible, and despite a language problem and unfamiliarity with urban life (he came from a rural area), this man achieved at a level above the university average.

FINANCIAL AID

The minority and low-income student, burdened by inferior preparedness, needs adequate financial aid so that he may devote himself fully to his studies. He cannot succeed in college if he must work fifteen or more hours a week. Finances must be provided.

The major sources of finance for disadvantaged students at Berkeley are federal grants and loans, some private gifts, university registration fees, and special regents' appropriations. The federal programs providing resources are Work-Study, Educational Opportunity Grants, and National Defense Education Act loans. These programs supply the bulk of funds for Berkeley's EOP students. The Educational Opportunity Grant program is being used to benefit many students who come from poverty circumstances as defined by the federal criterion. Educational Opportunity Grants aid entering freshmen of exceptional financial need, who for lack of financial means would otherwise be unable to enter or remain in college. The Work-Study program provides part-time employment for college students who need work to stay in college, with preference going to students from low-income families. Employment is limited to either on- or off-campus public or nonprofit organizations. Even application fees may be waived when necessary. Educational Opportunity Program freshmen are offered full-time jobs in the summer so they need not work during the school year. The goal is financial independence for the EOP student.

Great promise for overcoming financial barriers for disadvantaged students inheres in the stipulations of the federal Educational Opportunity Grant program. The program specifies that colleges are eligible for Educational Opportunity Grant funds only if they establish a vigorous recruiting program to identify and enroll disadvantaged students. However, many colleges with such programs receive EOG money and use it to match scholarship funds. Scholarships generally do not benefit minority group youth. In fact, more scholarship money goes to youth from families in the upper 15 percent financial bracket than to those in the bottom 40 percent. Stricter enforcement of the specifications of federal programs would serve to allocate increased financial resources to disadvantaged students.

A Student Needs Subcommittee has recommended to

the Centennial Fund Priorities Committee that fund raising for financially disadvantaged students be given the highest priority. A good program for both under-graduate and graduate students would require a mini-mum of five million dollars a year. A fund of $800,000 in university resources is currently available, matching two million dollars of federal and extramural funds.

EVALUATION

The Berkeley Educational Opportunity Program has been successful. One independent evaluation of Berke-ley's Educational Opportunity Program by the Southern Education Foundation characterizes the University of California as "the State University that appears to be 'getting with it' more than any other" in recruiting and aiding minority and low-income youth who show promise but do not fully meet admission requirements. Students in the program have done acceptable college work. Almost 70 percent of them are in good academic stand-ing with C-or-better grades. The remaining 30 percent are on academic probation with below-C grades. Signifi-cantly, the 60 percent of EOP students who were spe-cially admitted to the university have achieved as well as the others who were regularly admitted. The level of persistence has also been noteworthy. Of the 449 EOP freshmen admitted in 1967–1968, nearly 89 percent re-turned for the fall quarter, 1968, and of the 245 transfer students admitted the same year, 91 percent returned. The figure for spring, 1970, was 90 percent. The low attrition rate and the adequate academic performance constitute a very encouraging sign of success.

A longitudinal analysis of the student population indicates that the representation of low-income groups at the university is increasing. Just over 7 percent of those eligible to enroll in the university in the fall of 1967 came from families with an annual income of $6,000 or less. The corresponding figure for the fall of 1968 was 12 percent. The figure for spring, 1971, was 14 percent. Progress is definitely being made in increasing the enrollment of low-income students.

There are, unfortunately, some deficiencies and dysfunctions in the Berkeley Educational Opportunity Program. Academic tutoring for minority students is a major problem. A minimum of one part-time adviser is desirable for every ten students. Applying this formula, a program of academic assistance for minority students presently enrolled would cost at least $250,000. Yet funds are not available. Another problem is Government retrenchment on the Work-Study program. Only 60 percent of the requested funds were allocated in 1971. The 841 positions originally filled in fall, 1970, were cut to 598 for eleven rather than twelve weeks for the winter and spring quarters. The 90 noncampus community agencies and 135 campus employers involved in the program had their allotments reduced for winter and spring. An additional three hundred requests that cannot be filled are on file.

A very real threat to the higher education of the disadvantaged is the University of California's adoption of a six-hour entrance examination for all high school applicants. These tests, shown to be culturally biased, complicate the process of reaching minority and low-income persons. The so-called "culturally deprived" do very poorly on them. However, the adoption of flexible university entrance requirements in the spring of 1971 has rendered the tests less of a threat to significant minority representation on campus.

The California political climate also threatens Berkeley's program for the disadvantaged. There is great political opposition to admitting more minority students who do not meet admission standards. A recent poll showed only 13 percent of Californians approved of special admission for blacks. University of California President Charles J. Hitch has stated that "we must help make clear that special admission of black students is not leading to a lowering of our instructional standards. . . . In fact, the relatively good performance of many specially admitted students indicates that our admission standards need not be lowered so much as revised to be better predictors of college success." It is hoped that this argument can be carried effectively to the people and the state government. The degree to which the message reaches home will be a substantial determinant of the quality of race relations in California.

B. BERKELEY'S ETHNIC STUDIES COLLEGE

Black demands for better education became confrontation issues at the University of California at Berkeley during the fall of 1969. From the tension and painful dialogue at the time emerged a plan for an Ethnic Studies College that is now being implemented. The following analysis * of the Ethnic Studies College, written during

---

* Originally appeared in *Integrated Education,* Vol. VII, No. 4 (July–Aug., 1969), pp. 17–23. Reprinted by permission.

the 1969 controversy, points to both the institutional means and certain need for updating the university curricula in response to minority demands.

The recent proposal for an Ethnic Studies College at the University of California's Berkeley campus is an institutional response to both intramural and extramural pressures. On the intramural level, the Berkeley Academic Senate formally supported the establishment of an Ethnic Studies College and sponsored an interim Department of Ethnic Studies. The department is to begin in the fall of 1969, and will evolve into the Ethnic Studies College. The Senate also appointed a faculty advisory committee to counsel the chancellor concerning the development of the department. The committee has been instructed to submit names of candidates for the department chairmanship. Extramurally, student agitation—both white and minority—made a major campus issue of "Third World" curricula.

STUDENTS STRIKE

The Third World student strike brought a gubernatorial state of emergency to the Berkeley campus in January, 1969. Police have been on campus in large numbers ever since in a continuing state of emergency. The ensuing confrontation between police and students has been marked by violence on both sides, arrests, and even tear gas to disperse crowds. More characteristically, the student advocates of an Ethnic Studies College have spoken to campus living groups, published leaflets, and negotiated with representatives of the university administration to move toward a workable solution. From this dialogue—generated by intramural and extramural spokesmen, and however limited at times—emerged the plan for an Ethnic Studies College at Berkeley.

The Ethnic Studies College, as proposed by minority students and faculty, will focus on minority peoples' problems in both rural and urban settings. The curriculum will be oriented to producing scholars who can deal effectively with contemporary minority problems. To achieve this, the college will be considerably more community-oriented than a traditional academic department.

The Ethnic Studies College will have its own administrative officials and its own regulations for obtaining degrees. All students must satisfy degree requirements on university, college, and field of concentration levels. The Ethnic Studies student may elect a double major, single major, or Ethnic Studies major. The double major consists of majoring in one of the fields offered in the college and a field outside the college. For example, a student may major in Afro-American Studies and Sociology or Asian Studies and Economics. The single major focuses exclusively upon an area of study within the college (Asian-American, Afro-American, Native American, or Mexican-American Studies). The Ethnic Studies major allows the student to become knowledgeable in two or more fields of study offered within the college. Since many substantive issues that will be the concern of the Ethnic Studies College are related to social scientific theoretical approaches and research, cooperative and collaborative relationships with such departments as sociology, psychology, and anthropology can be developed.

First Two Years

During the freshman and sophomore years, the Ethnic Studies student takes an introductory series of courses. The Afro-American Studies student, for example, takes a series of courses which provide an overview of the black experience from economic, historical, political, and sociological perspectives. The courses include Racism, Colonialism, and Apartheid, Economics of Racism, Urbanization of Black People, and Psychology of Racism. In the junior year, the student declares his area of specialization. He may elect, for example, to concentrate in the sociology of the black family. In conjunction with his course work, the student devotes the second and third quarters of his junior year to field work. Assisted by a faculty member of the Afro-American Studies Program, the student researches some problem consistent with his area of concentration. The basic research methodology is participant observation. The first quarter of the senior year is spent in a seminar with other seniors who have been in the field. The seminar is conducted by the faculty of the Afro-American Studies Program. During the second and third quarters, the student prepares his senior dissertation based upon his field experiences. Upon successful completion of the program, the student is awarded the Bachelor of Arts degree in Afro-American Studies.

In addition to the four-year curriculum for the B.A. outlined above, the Ethnic Studies College will offer courses in community-based, extension, and experimental programs. The college will offer courses in ethnic studies to minority communities. The location and content of the courses will be developed in coordination with various local organizations and groups. The college will offer, on a limited basis, courses through the University of California Extension Educational Program. Students are also encouraged to develop courses in their own areas of interest. These can possibly be accredited through the university's experimental course provisions.

FEDERALISM AND SEPARATISM

The Third World Liberation Front (TWLF), representing nonwhite, minority students, wants the Ethnic Studies College faculty to be entirely of minority scholars and the students to be almost solely from minority backgrounds. This request cannot, however, be translated into policy because of the legal statutes against segregated education, particularly when federal monies are involved. The TWLF's demand that students admitted to the Ethnic Studies College receive necessary financial, counseling, and tutoring assistance is more feasible.

The Ethnic Studies College will also include the recently established, interdisciplinary Institute of Race and Community Relations. The institute studies contemporary inter-ethnic relations, minority social problems, and racial conflict. The research is applied by the institute's Community Program Center to help off-campus groups in race and community relations. It also engages in educational work and assists community groups in securing resources.

In submitting a proposal for an Ethnic Studies College, the Third World Liberation Front at Berkeley demanded an education more relevant to the sociocultural background of minority students. It asked for Afro-American, Native American, Chicano (Mexican-American), and

Asian curricula. These curricula will be offered in the "Third World College," as the TWLF prefers to call the Ethnic Studies College. The TWFL conceives of the college's purpose as follows:

> The goal of the Third World College will be to provide an education of the highest quality while allowing students to retain their cultural identity, thus enabling them to return to their communities to live and to create an atmosphere conducive to political, social, and economic changes.

New Based on Old

The concept of an academic structure devoted to both intellectual pursuits and social action is not new at Berkeley. The application of knowledge to minority community problems does not, therefore, represent in form anything particularly new. The Center for Real Estate and Urban Economics, for example, does research such as the "Application of Land-Use Simulation Models for Regional Forecasting." The innovative aspects of the Ethnic Studies College are the substantive concerns to which faculty and students address themselves. Minority relations as an academic specialty is unsettling to a public accustomed to relatively detached institutions of higher learning. A college committed to minority study and uplift is particularly disconcerting to a society where colleges and universities have been traditionally bastions of a subtle and persistent form of white supremacy. Hence, one finds the California public's immediate reaction expressed in a recent survey where only 13 percent felt that promising blacks should be admitted by special provision to the university.

The local conditions and historical details surrounding the incipient development of Berkeley's Ethnic Studies College should not obscure the underlying principle that university curricula ought to be increasingly socially relevant. Dramatic and unfortunate events brought the issue of "Third World studies" into prominence in the campus dialogue. The faculty and administration then began to listen seriously to the demands for internal curricular reform that were at their doorstep—some, if for no other reason than that the tear gas and the strike had emptied their classes and offices. As a consequence, they initiated a genuine effort to incorporate ethnic studies into the curriculum.

The lesson that should have been learned at Berkeley (time will tell) is that student initiation of courses should be legitimized and institutionalized so that potentially explosive confrontations need not occur. Provisions should be made for the continuing updating of the university experience. Cultural lag should never become so pronounced among a community of scholars that frustration and anger prevail over rational inquiry and compassionate understanding.

Conclusion

The minority demands for quality education challenge the American rhetoric of equal opportunity. The meritocracy requires formal education, often for substantially certification purposes, but usually involving some learning that is valuable in the marketplace. Red, brown, and black Americans must enjoy access to excellent education if they are to compete successfully and earn their share of the good things of life, both as a function of their becoming certificated and learning high-level skills. To deny the minorities either access to better education or participation in shaping the curriculum, and, ultimately, appropriate jobs, puts a severe strain on the capacity of the social system to prevent their aspiration from turning to bitterness and violence. This turn of events, perhaps culminating in the destruction of a nation, must be avoided at all costs.

Humanity is really a unity. Prejudice and discrimination have tragically cut gaping wounds in the community of men for centuries. The negative product of disunity, past and present, in terms of both the psychological and physical quality of life, has been staggering. The loss to the United States of unfulfilled minority demands for better education extends the historic tragedy. When oppressed men cannot inform their idiosyncratic experiences with the wisdom of their forebears and are unable to learn the technical skills to carry on productive employment, both the intellectual sophistication of the population is depressed, which has extremely negative implications for democratic politics, and the percentage of citizens on welfare increases, which portends ill for our economic system of free enterprise. Therefore, from both humanistic and material perspectives, the satisfaction of minority demands for better education is imperative.

Finally, red, brown, and black Americans are not the only economically and educationally disadvantaged Americans. Two thirds of all Americans who are so disadvantaged are white. It is clear that red, brown, and black demands for better education are also the demands of impoverished whites. Skin color, in the last analysis, is irrelevant. The only consideration should be that wherever there is suffering there should also be compassion. Moral concern alone should be sufficient to move us to accommodate the legitimate educational aspirations and needs of red, brown, and black Americans who happen to suffer most grievously the injustice of our particular social system. Only if we act resolutely upon the ideal that men everywhere share the same fate, and that the diminishment of one is the desecration of all, will red, brown, and black people, as well as all whites, be able to make their unique contribution to our society, learning what they will where, when, and how they will and doing a work that accommodates their talents and satisfies their aspirations.

Appendix
Third World Liberation
Front Documents

The Third World Liberation Front at the University of California at Berkeley, a coalition of minority students, initiated a strike in 1969 in support of the establishment of an Ethnic Studies College. That confrontation is described in section 12 A in this book, "Berkeley's Ethnic Studies College." During and following the crisis, red, brown, and black students expressed numerous demands for better education. The three fliers presented here articulate the basic thrust of Native American, Mexican-American, and Afro-American students' demands. The Third World Liberation Front distributed these fliers at the Sather Gate entrance to the Berkeley campus, from which point they eventually found their way into the Social Protest Archives of the Bancroft Library. I selected these three as most representative of the 147 items that have been collected on the Third World Liberation Front.

A. WHAT THE RED STUDENT WANTS

HISTORY—PHILOSOPHY—DIRECTION

Retrospectively, Native American Studies have been in existence for only a brief period of time as a separate academic discipline within but a few colleges and universities throughout the country. This is in diametric opposition to the ancient past of the natives of this continent. It has become increasingly apparent that the ethnocentric insularity perpetuated in the Anglo-American educational system has to be combated through studies of the minorities of this country, a country which once belonged solely to the natives of this continent to which others were welcomed in a spirit of friendship.

Native American Studies at the University of California, Berkeley, has been in existence as a Program since 1969, and was a direct result of the Third World Liberation Front Strike in 1969. This strike paralyzed the day-to-day operations of the University, and was successful in that the Department of Ethnic Studies was created as an interim department. Native American Studies is one of four programs within this Department along with Afro-American Studies, Asian American Studies, and Chicano Studies.

Presently the Native American Studies Program has a faculty consisting of five lecturers, and has several people employed as staff members, who are in charge of the daily operations of the Program Office. In addition, there are approximately fifty American Indian students. Collectively, the faculty, staff, and students come from all parts of the nation and represent numerous American Indian tribes.

By learning to combine classroom experience and actual community activity within American Indian structures, new and innovative approaches to community projects are being developed. Tutoring Indian children in East Oakland and working with Indian inmates in San Quentin and the California Medical Facility, Vacaville, are two examples of the experience emphasized within the Program. Also, included in the experiences of students are lecturing to public schools and supervising a Native American Studies class in the New Community High School of Oakland.

It is anticipated that the ultimate result of Native American Studies at the University of California, Berkeley, will be to negate the one-sided picture of the American Indian, which has too often been that of the forever faithful companion of Lone Ranger, or the stoic image of the Indian smoking his peace pipe. Through Native American Studies, the Native Americans are able to present their own side of the picture, the picture of truth and the knowledge of their historical development as a nation of peoples.

The direction of Native American Studies is to develop into a unit of academic excellence in the tradition of the University of California at Berkeley. It is recognized that the needs of Native Americans on a nation-wide level are such that Native American Studies must continue to encourage the development of a strong core of professional people to work directly with our peoples in the areas of education, social work, medicine, law, and so on. On one level of development, Native American Studies is developing a minor so that the Native American student can be provided with a knowledge and understanding of his people, thereby allowing him to specialize in those areas where there is still and will continue to be a great need.

A second level of development is that Native American Studies will develop an A.B. degree granting program with a major in Native American Studies. Those students who major in Native American Studies will be provided with a comprehensive yet highly specialized training in the areas of American Indian community development, history, education, languages, and general liberal arts. Simultaneously, Native American Studies will evolve into a Department housed within a Third World College along with the three other components of Afro-American Studies, Asian-American Studies, and Chicano Studies.

Another projection is the development of a Center of Native American Studies housed within the Institute of Race and Community Relations, which will function as an extension of Native American Studies. This Center will provide the Native American with the opportunity to conduct intensive, scholarly, and sophisticated research, as well as providing funds for long-range community oriented programs.

Through courses taught from an Indian perspective by top level Indian personnel, Native American Studies at the University of California, Berkeley, is dedicated to the education of the native of this continent, as well as to the education of the non-Indian student of this nation. This objective is reflective of the attitude of the Native American, in general, that education is the key to our survival as a people.

Native Americans,
Third World Liberation Front
(Filed in Social Protest Archives,
Bancroft Library, Berkeley, November 5, 1970)

B. WHAT THE BROWN STUDENT WANTS

A THIRD WORLD COLLEGE
(To Include a Department of Chicano Studies)
A CHICANO CENTER
AN EXTENSION PROGRAM

This is a proposal and a recommendation for the establishment of a Chicano Department within the Third World College. The Chicano Department is envisioned as undergoing two stages of development. First, it will be established as a Division within an interim independent Department of Third World Studies. Second, it will subsequently become a Department within the Third World College. Since the substance of the Departmental Division closely parallels the College Department, primary focus in what follows is oriented to the second proposed developmental step.

From the U.S. Commission on Civil Rights, to the local barrio, the need for more involvement of the Chicano community has been amply documented. The question that is most salient now addresses itself to what response will come from public institutions of higher education, such as the University of California at Berkeley.

The present needs of the Chicano must be met in such a way as to provide relevant programs which will sustain self-confidence and provide a feeling of acceptance on the student's terms. Furthermore, such a response must also surpass the traditional boundaries of academe by providing a "home base" as it were, in the form of housing, assistance, social life, etc. Very importantly, bilingual studies must constitute a part of the University's realistic recognition of community realities and innovative academic potential. Clearly a part of the function of a department must be to prepare students for more advanced participation in the University outside the Chicano Department; i. e., study pattern assistance, use of library, cultural and behavioral patterns of the dominant society, etc. Financial assistance that takes into account the student's obligation is needed, as well as highly competent counseling by Chicanos.

INTRODUCTION

Third World Americans have long been aware of the bias of Anglo-American universities and thus it is not at all surprising that the various Third World groups, including especially students of non-white origin, have been ordinarily far ahead of Anglo-American faculty and administrators in perceiving the need for fundamental change. This situation has led to "confrontation" at various institutions, confrontations which could in almost every case have been avoided if Third World groups themselves, at an early stage, had been provided with the means for diversifying the courses and programs. That this is a procedure to be recommended seems rather clear in view of both the psychological need of oppressed persons for some degree of control over their own educational destiny and the inability of most faculty and administrators to reform their own programs voluntarily.

In many areas of the nation programs are now being developed which focus upon only one community (especially Afro-Americans) but in other areas the needs of other Third World groups demand the creation of diversified, multi-ethnic programs. Colleges and schools of "Ethnic Studies" or "Third World Studies" are now being proposed to encompass the needs of the Third World communities in multi-ethnic sections of the country.

THE SIGNIFICANCE AND SCOPE
OF THIRD WORLD STUDIES

At the time of the War for United States Independence the Atlantic Seaboard population (exclusive of Indian areas and Florida) was about 25% non-European, while the balance of the area of the present-day United States was predominantly Native American or mixed Native American European, and African (New Mexico, Florida, and lower Louisiana). As European immigrants rushed in the percentage of non-whites gradually declined but it has seldom dropped below 20% (where it stands today). The proportion of non-Anglos is rapidly increasing once again, with the Asian-American, the Native American, the Spanish-speaking, and the Afro-American populations all possessing much higher birthrates than the Euro-American majority. In California, for example, Third World people constitute about 20–22% of the total population and about 25% of the school-age population.

Clearly, the history, culture, and affairs of all of America's people prior to the European invasion and from one-fourth to one-fifth of the United States' population since the seventeenth-century demand detailed study in terms of instructional programs, research, and community services. Furthermore, one can cite the fact that perhaps one-half of the peoples of the Americas as a whole are today of Native American, African, Asian, or mixed descent (and, of course, that the majority of the world's people are of non-European origin) to illustrate the significance of Third World Studies.

One must also stress these additional points: (1) that the United States' Third World communities possess the greatest needs of any sector of the population in terms of conceiving higher education as oriented towards the service of the nation; (2) that inter-ethnic relations, and the problems of race and color, loom as the most significant "problem area" for the contemporary United States; (3) that well-documented objective needs exist for teachers, social workers, community workers, inter-group relations specialists and other professionals of Third World and non-Third World origin who are extremely well-trained in terms of the history, culture, and conditions of Third World communities; (4) that the world's Third World populations and non-European majorities possess great needs which can be, in part, met by Third World-oriented higher education; (5) that inter-ethnic relations ("frontiers") and the problems of race and color are crucial in the existing relations between nation-states and within the boundaries of multi-national states; and (6) that well-documented needs exist for persons trained to work with inter-ethnic relations at the international level and with overseas Third World populations.

The Wisdom of a College Structure

A separate college is herein recommended as the most suitable vehicle for a Third World studies program, for the following reasons:

(1) Most existing university faculties and departments have had a century or more in which to develop multi-ethnic approaches to history, art, literature, education, and so on, but they have been largely unable to do so because of their own ethnocentric, "culture-bound" values as well as because of the "built-in" preconceptions of their respective disciplines. These same faculties cannot now be expected to do what they have in the past rejected or failed to consider as "academically worthy" subjects.

(2) The area of Third World studies and inter-ethnic analysis has suffered from the fact that the disciplines theoretically concerned with this field (sociology, anthropology, psychology, and so on) have tended to develop highly specialized methodologies or approaches which have seldom allowed for a systematic, interdisciplinary focus on problems of ethnicity as such. For example, inter-ethnic rivalries and ethnic dynamics comprise a large part of the substance of so-called international relations, but the discipline of international relations largely ignores cultural and ethnic dynamics in order to concentrate upon legal-institutional analyses. It would appear that only an integrated ethnic studies program can overcome the above problems.

(3) A Third World studies program, to be meaningful, must embrace basic research (theoretical as well as empirical), applied research, and extensive field training.

Because of these factors such a program does not belong in the College of Letters and Sciences. A Third World studies program must be regarded as being comparable to the programs of the College of Agriculture (with its applied research and field activities), the School of Social Welfare, the School of Education, or the School of Medicine.

A Third World studies program without its applied aspect would be like the School of Education without Teacher Education, Boalt Hall without courtroom practice, or the School of Medicine without internship experiences.

Basic research cannot, however, be ignored since so many of the needs of Third World peoples cannot be fully met until tools are available. For example, the need for Black-oriented textbooks in the secondary schools cannot be fully met until long-neglected aspects of Black history are fully revealed by intensive research.

(4) The faculty for a Third World studies program will have to possess varying kinds of expertise. Many will doubtlessly be persons who could qualify for appointments in the College of Letters and Sciences, but others will be practitioners comparable to faculties of Schools of Education, Law, etc. The doctorate does not make a person qualified to teach in the area of Native American Community Development, for example. Such an instructor should rather have had some years of applied experience in addition to an understanding of the theory of cultural change and community organization.

(5) The creation of specialized programs (as with Schools of Medicine, Law, etc.) always demands that the larger community of experts outside of the normal faculty be drawn upon to assist with their expertise and

practical experience. A School of Medicine would hardly be established without the active collaboration of the several appropriate medical organizations, and the same would be true with Law, Agriculture, and other fields. A Third World studies program is similar, in the sense that few faculty and administrators have had the kind of training or experience necessary for a real understanding of the applied and field aspects of the subject area. Therefore, it would seem clear that a Third World studies program cannot be established in the way that a department within the College of Letters and Sciences would normally be initiated. The community of experts which must be drawn upon (Third World students and leading representatives from Third World communities) clearly indicates the need for a college-type structure allowing naturally for supra-faculty participation in planning.

(6) The distinction between a "School" and a "College" according to the Standing Orders of the Regents precludes the establishment of a "School" since a "School" may not enroll lower-division students.

In summary, a college-type of structure would seem to be indicated by the reality of the existing organization at Berkeley, by the very nature of the concept of Third World studies, and by the necessity for the involvement of experts from beyond the range of normal faculty.

THE DEPARTMENT OF CHICANO STUDIES

The concept of a bilingual program or department is not new. The University of the Pacific has had a bilingual College for many years, although its purpose when established was to relate to the Spanish-speaking countries of the Americas. Texas A & I University has bilingual programs in its School of Agriculture, School of Business Administration, and School of Engineering. And there are others.

Bilingual programs are designed to meet the developmental needs of the students and of the communities to which they relate. Not only are perceptions and academic styles distinct, but instruction is given in both Spanish and English.

LOWER DIVISION

Goals of the first two years are to develop students' abilities in a bilingual, bicultural manner by offering communication skills in both Spanish and English, by focusing on an intellectual perspective of and about the Spanish-speaking communities, and by establishing a sound basis from which the student may select his major either in the Department or outside of it after two years.

The development of courses should remain flexible, although at this time there are the following possibilities:

(1) Rhetoric and Communication Skills:
       Spanish   1–6 quarters
(2) Rhetoric and Communication Skills:
       English   1–6 quarters
(3) Contemporary Community Problems   3 quarters
(4) Historical Culture
       of the Spanish-speaking   3 quarters
(5) Styles of Expression, Creativity,
       Arts   3 quarters
(6) Cultural Economics   3 quarters

(7) Political Constraints: Education,
    Crime, Welfare, etc.   3 quarters
(8) Technological Symbols and Concepts   1–3 quarters

UPPER DIVISION

Goals for the major are to develop students' abilities to serve their communities, and to develop a potential for self-fulfillment in at least two cultures.

Courses will offer field work, directed research, supervised teaching and counseling, etc., as well as the conventional classes on campus. The programming will depend upon the student's abilities and needs so that it would be possible, for example, for a student to be on campus for the fall quarter, then go to the Central Valley for the winter quarter, return to the campus for the spring quarter, then to the barrios for the summer. The important inter-relationship of the Department, the Center, and the Extension program would be an important factor in developing viable individualization of instruction.

Since the Department of Chicano Studies would offer a limited number of courses, majors in this field would have the opportunity and need to go to existing departments in other Colleges and Schools to complete graduation requirements. There are many courses already given that would be recommended in such fields as Social Welfare, Criminology, Public Health, Anthropology, Political Science, etc. Furthermore, students would be encouraged to take courses in the other Third World departments, as well as the core courses for all Third World groups.

Suggested possible courses:

(1) Linguistics and Dialectology
(2) Consumer Education
(3) Health, Education and Welfare
(4) Government, Civil Rights, etc.
(5) Social Institutions
(6) Ideology and Philosophy
(7) Communication, Translation
(8) Mass Media, Journalism
(9) Literature of the Spanish-speaking
(10) Performing Arts
(11) Plastic Arts
(12) Comparative Third World Studies
(13) International Third World Studies
(14) Third World Strategies
(15) Cybernetics and the Third World

THE CHICANO BILINGUAL CENTER

Absolutely essential to the development of a Chicano Curriculum, a Chicano Extension Program, and adequate involvement in the Urban Crisis Program is the establishment of an adequately supported Chicano Center. The reasons for this are many: (1) A program is needed to gather, classify, and make available the increasing number of published and unpublished materials relating to the Chicano population. This can take the form of a specialized library as a part of the center. (2) Closely related to this effort is a program of research analysis whose task it will be to evaluate on-going research findings, and to assist in translating these findings into a meaningful form so that they may be used to assist in the development of teaching materials as well as in the development of community programs. (3) While the fore-going is a program to *gather* research, there should also be a program to *initiate* research; that is, to articulate research problems in a manner that is relevant to the Chicano community. Such efforts will also be directed towards assistance for research-oriented students in the Department of Chicano Studies. (4) The Center will also assist in the development of Extension Programs, either rural or urban. (5) The Center should also address itself to the need of a Cultural Events Program. (6) The demand for speakers is growing daily. The availability of speakers, and their areas of special knowledge, should be coordinated by the Centers. (7) The Center should be prepared to provide assistance to schools. (8) Scholars in Residence programs should be developed in order to tap the broad talents of the Chicano community.

AN EXTENSION PROGRAM

The University of California Extension Programs were placed on a self-sustaining basis when State funds were withdrawn. The consequence of this act was to limit participation in Extension programs to members of the affluent and professional sectors of the citizenry.

Since Chicano communities hardly belong to the aforementioned groups, the University's Extension programs have excluded Chicanos from any of its activities. It is recommended, therefore, that the University fund Extension programs under the jurisdiction of the Chicano Department (Third World College) from its Urban Crisis and other sources.

Two types of programs can be envisioned initially. One would be of direct service to meet the needs of

Chicano communities, probably analogous to Agricultural Extension. For example, the problem of housing among the farm workers is a serious one. The other would be somewhat similar to conventional Extension classes, except that the "teaching" staff would include advanced students from the Chicano Department and community experts in the field, or wherever the students would feel most comfortable and non-alienated. Furthermore, classes would be offered at the pre-university levels as well as at university levels. This is essential in order to recoup some of the students who were "pushed out" of primary and secondary schools.

> The Mexican-American Student Confederation and
> The Third World Liberation Front
> (Filed in Social Protest Archives,
> Bancroft Library, Berkeley, February 9, 1969)

C. WHAT THE BLACK STUDENT WANTS

WE ARE NOT ASKING, WE ARE DEMANDING

The young Black people of America are the inheritors of what is undoubtedly one of the most challenging, grave, and threatening set of social circumstances that has ever fallen upon a generation of young people anywhere in history. We have been born into a hostile and alien society which loathes us on condition of our skin color. Our intimidated and frightened parents, not less but more victimized, have been unable to tell us why. Sentenced to inaneness, subservience, and death, from our beginning, many of us came to regard our beautiful pigmentation as a plague. It should surprise no one that the first thing we discovered was our "souls," as we were so bare and totally lacking anything else. Unless there be reason for mis-understanding—let us make it clear that we neither cry nor complain to anyone about being left with our "souls," because the soul is sufficient unto itself. We act now because we realize, beyond any doubt, that our "souls," i.e., that which is all and the end of us, have been stifled to the point that we can no longer bear it. We have been forced to the point where we must (and will) insist on those changes that are necessary to our survival. There is nothing less to settle for and nothing less will do.

The college and university campuses of America are a long way from where most of us come. Our homeland (known to white folks as the GHETTO) is hardly conducive to the growing of ivy. "Mother wits" was our thing, not encyclopedias. We have been the companions of every evil, cycle, syndrome, or mania that would strike fear in the hearts of our white compatriots. Those of us who survive have seen everything but the end. This many of us stayed by trekking from our homeland to your midst; to your college and university campuses. We could not have imagined what awaited us.

As students on the white college and university campuses of America we have learned something which we choose never to forget.

WE ARE NOT WHITE. WE DO NOT WISH TO BE WHITE. WHAT IS GOOD FOR WHITE PEOPLE IS OFTENTIMES WORSE THAN BAD FOR US.

Education in America, as we have come to know it, is a strictly utilitarian endeavor. The colleges and universities have not been established for the sake of education. The colleges and universities are the wholesale producers of a designated mentality conducive to the perpetuation and continuation of America's present national life. A national life which we have witnessed to be in total and complete contradiction to the wholesome development and survival of our people. There is little need to detail the sad circumstances of our plight in American society. This tale is already well known. Not even the blind and insane could deny or refute the unspeakable horrors that America has wrought upon its citizens of color. Finally, we have witnessed white America's long overdue self-admittance of its racism. Thus, knowing and recognizing fully the gravity of the circumstances under which we labor, we are moving to institute all those changes prerequisite to our survival in an openly hostile country. While our elders share the burden of these circumstances, it is clear to us that this is a burden too great for them to shoulder alone; that we, the young, must shoulder the major portion of this burden; that we, the young, are the key link to the survival of our kind; that we must therefore call unto and surround ourselves with resources of all kinds and material which will aid us in preparing for this great task. A qualitative change in our education is necessary to this end.

The black student in America has, for as long as anyone can remember, been the victim of mental brutality, character subversion, and inundatory alienation from his black community. His value to his community at the end of his college or university career has been *zero*. His community has thereby been left without the element most essential to its regeneration and reconstruction—its awake young people. Black students can no longer afford to be educated away from their origins. Henceforth, our education must speak to the needs of our community and our people. We can no longer prostitute our minds to the vain and irrelevant intellectual pursuits of Western society while our community lies in ruin and our people are threatened with concentration camps. This would amount to intellectual shuffling and we are determined to shuffle no more.

It is important to note here that our proposal is not a product of reaction. We are well beyond reaction. We are addressing ourselves to a basic change of attitude. This change is primarily a product of self discovery. A kind of self discovery which has snatched our minds from the rank of a historically insignificant, persecuted minority and placed us among the world's majority populace which is crying from one end of the earth to the other that "we are." We are decided that we alone can define ourselves, that we are beautiful despite the white negative concept of us, that we have a history, an art, and a culture, that no race or nation can stamp out our "souls" no matter the intensity of this foolish effort.

We must therefore ask with unrelenting insistence that our future education be radically reformed. We demand a program of "BLACK STUDIES," a program which will be of, by, and for black people. We demand that we be educated realistically; and that no form of education which attempts to lie to us, or otherwise mis-educate us will be accepted.

If the university *is not* prepared to educate us in such a way that our education may be relative to our lives, then we demand that the university prepare itself to do so immediately. If the university *will not* prepare itself to address our educational needs, then we demand that the university accept no more of our parents' tax money which it has used in the past to mis-educate us.

The Afro-American Student Union and
The Third World Liberation Front
(Filed in Social Protest Archives,
Bancroft Library, Berkeley, February 4, 1969)